HARRELL FLETCHER

THE SOUND WE MAKE TOGETHER (MELBOURNE)

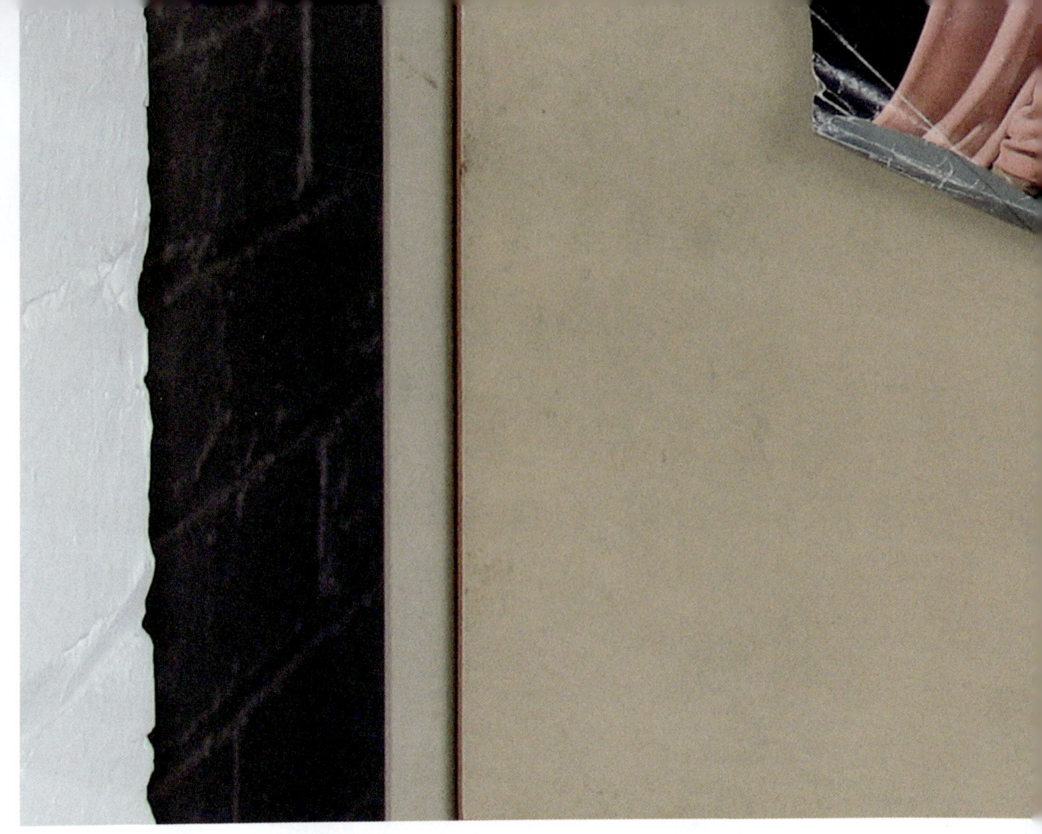

HARRELL FLETCHER

THE SOUND WE MAKE TOGETHER (MELBOURNE)

Arts Project Australia was founded in 1974 to nurture and promote artists with intellectual disabilities. Both a studio program and gallery, Arts Project Australia provides artists with professiona guidance, quality materials and a space to work and show their art. Arts Project Australia promotes and exhibits artists' work within the broad spectrum of contemporary art; studio artists are represented in mainstream art exhibitions fairs and other events. In addition, mainstream artists collaborate with Arts Project artists and show in the gallery, underscoring the resonance of studio artists to the world of contemporary art.

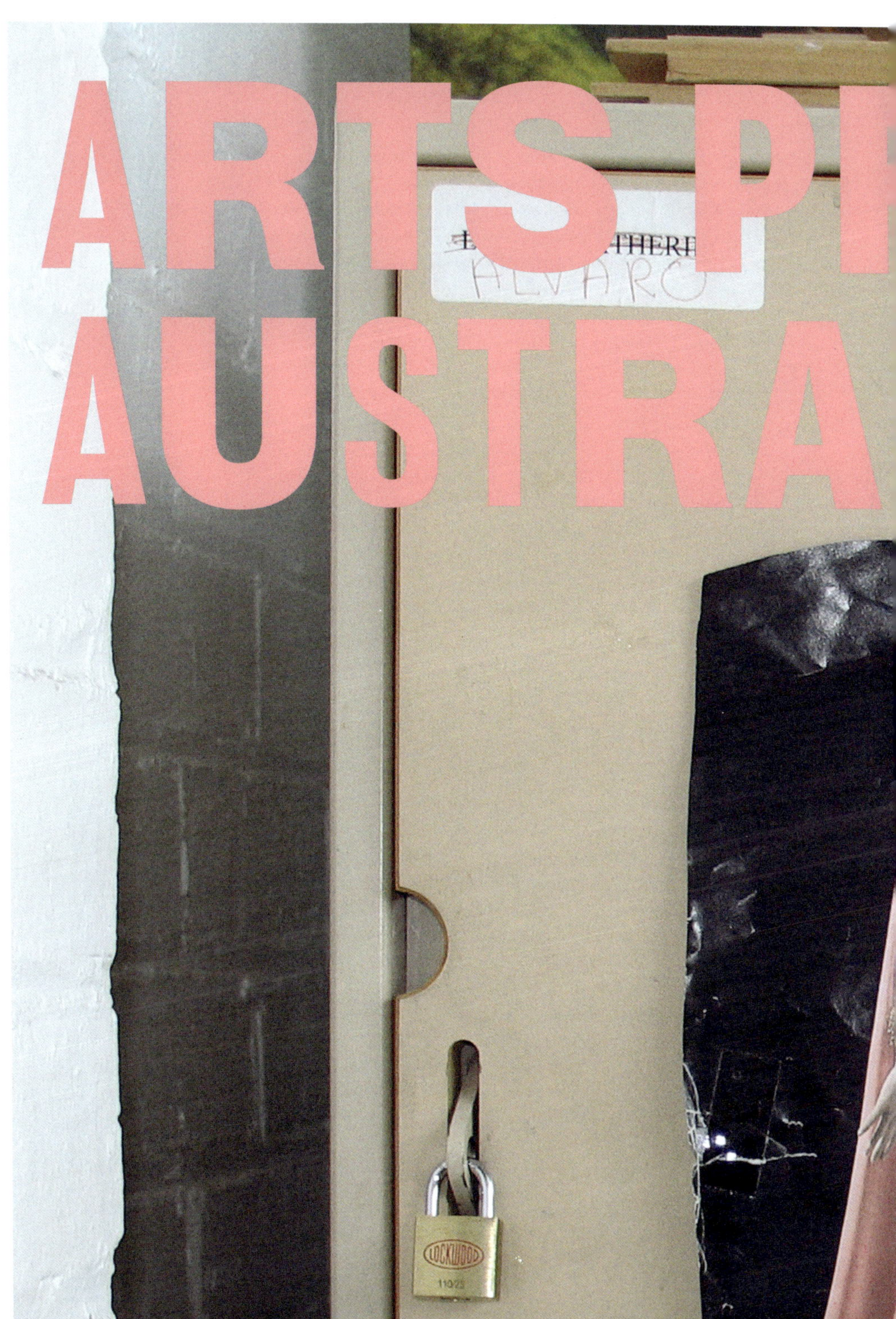
ARTS
AUSTRA
ALVARO
LOCKWOOD

Harrell Fletcher's practice is exceptional in the way it brings individuals and community organisations together in a spirit of collaboration. In *Harrell Fletcher: The Sound We Make Together (Melbourne)* he has gathered together individuals and community groups from across Melbourne and invited them collectively to contribute to the development of the exhibition. Fletcher and the curator of the project, our Senior Curator of Contemporary Art, Alex Baker, has worked with the selected groups and individuals including Arts Project Australia, CERES, Crooked Rib Art, Footscray Community Arts Centre, Grainger Museum, Hell Gallery, Herb Patten, Jeff Sparrow and RISE, to realise a singular reflection on contemporary and historical Melbourne. This expression has taken many forms including presentations, performances, photography, objects, printed ephemera and a selection of works of art from the National Gallery of Victoria collection chosen by each exhibitor.

The series of presentations and the resulting exhibition has opened up the professional world of curating to diverse community groups across Melbourne, inviting an alternative approach to exhibition making. It challenges our assumptions concerning the traditional role of the artist, the curator and the art museum by facilitating a democratic involvement in the various aspects of exhibition production.

Harrell Fletcher: The Sound We Make Together (Melbourne) highlights our commitment to fostering community engagement with the arts and with the NGV itself. We are delighted and deeply impressed by the energy and enthusiasm each participant has brought to the project, and feel privileged to have had the opportunity to work so closely with them. We hope to continue this initiative by presenting exhibitions and events in the future which actively encourage diverse engagement with the NGV by a broad section of the community.

I would like to extend my warmest thanks to Harrell Fletcher for his generosity and unique collaborative approach, enabling us to realise this remarkable exhibition. I sincerely thank all the community participants in the project: Arts Project Australia, CERES, Crooked Rib Art, Footscray Community Arts Centre, Grainger Museum, Hell Gallery, Herb Patten, Jeff Sparrow and RISE. Thanks must also be extended to Perpetual Philanthropic Services who have generously supported the exhibition. Finally, I would like to extend special acknowledgment to Alex Baker and the NGV team who have worked tirelessly with Harrell Fletcher and the local participants to bring to the NGV *Harrell Fletcher: The Sound We Make Together (Melbourne).*

Gerard Vaughan
Director, National Gallery of Victoria

Harrell Fletcher: The Sound We Make Together (Melbourne) has been a collaboration in the truest sense of the word. The exhibition has involved a range of participants in the Melbourne community, from individuals to organisations, some within the sphere of contemporary art and others in very different fields. The array of interests and ideas espoused by our collaborators in this exciting venture was exactly the aim of the project. The title of the exhibition conjures an image of a multiplicity of voices singing together: harmonic perfection is not so much the goal, rather the fact of gathering together and 'singing' in the very first place is.

I would like to thank all of our participants and collaborators: Sue Roff, Sim Luttin, Cheryl Daye, Lisa Reid and Paul Hodges of Arts Project Australia; Marg Vandeleur, Cinnamon Evans and Judy Glick of CERES; Crooked Rib Art, with a particular thanks to Reeham Hakem for handling our various requests and facilitating aspects of the project; Jennifer Barry and her team at Footscray Community Arts Centre including Michael Brennan, Bec Reid and Erin Watson; Astrid Krautschneider, Monica Syrette and Brian Allison of the Grainger Museum; Jess Johnson and Jordan Marani of Hell Gallery; Herb Patten; Ramesh Fernandez and Frank Mwamba of RISE; and Jeff Sparrow. Our participants devoted time and energy in a diversity of ways: the thought put into the loans of materials and objects; the making of works of art specifically for the exhibition; the selection of works of art from NGV storage; presenting lectures and performances for our weekend of presentations (and, in some cases, inviting guest artists and presenters); taking time to show us where and how they work or places significant to them. I thank you for your generosity in sharing your unique worlds with our NGV audience.

This project would not have been possible without Harrell Fletcher, whose way of working is singular in the field of contemporary art. Recognised for giving platforms to people to express their creative vision, Fletcher has the unusual ability to work within a given situation and organically develop projects that showcase the talents and interests of others. Fletcher recognised the important resources available both within the NGV and the Melbourne community and brought these elements together. He provided the structure for this project: that we invite participants to select works of art from the NGV collection in a hands-on way through visits to NGV storage; that we invite participants to make presentations to a gathered audience that would be video documented and then, later, be continuously

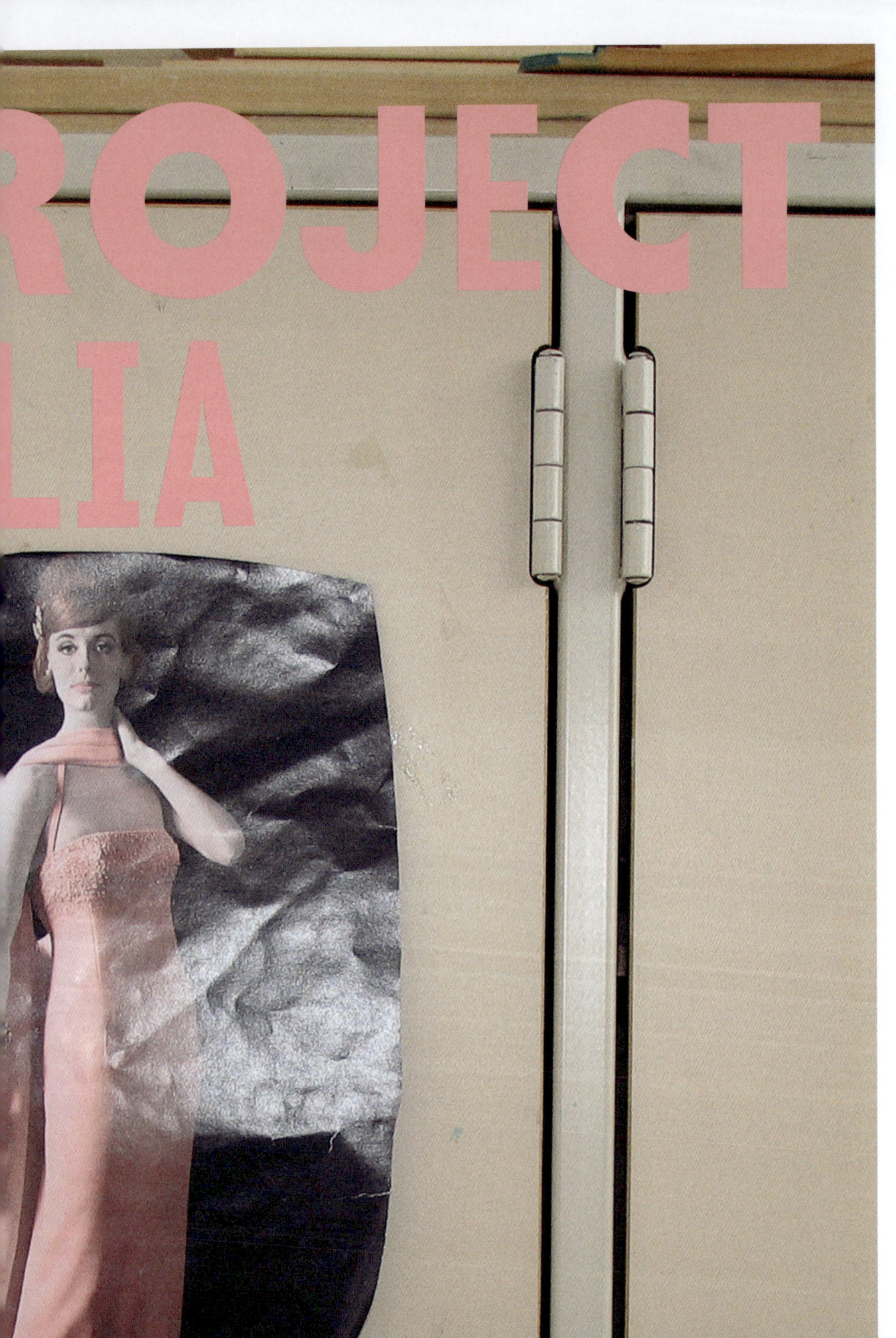
ROJECT
LIA

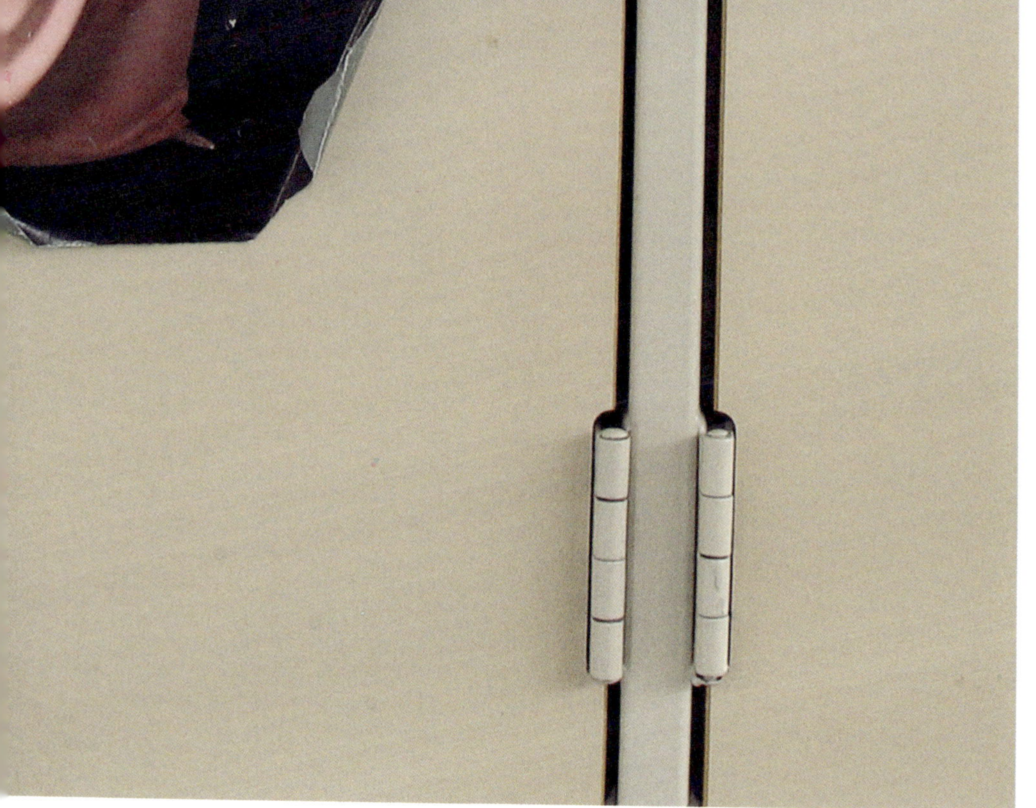

**11 SEP –
30 JAN 11**

Arts Project Australia
24 High Street
Northcote Victoria 3070
www.artsproject.org.au

Harrell Fletcher
Alvaro Alvarez's locker, Arts Project Australia 2010 (detail)
colour inkjet print
Collection of the artist,
Portland, Oregon

ngv
National
Gallery of
Victoria

screened in the exhibition space; that he would visit participants and photo-document their working environments – the resulting photographs would be juxtaposed with participants' selections from the NGV collection. Fletcher also suggested that each organisation and individual present themselves the best they could through the lending of ephemera, posters, books and works of art. Wearing the hat of artist, facilitator, curator and listener, Fletcher has envisioned a project that has dissolved distinctions between art and non-art objects; artists and non-artists – he makes it clear that art museums can aspire to inclusivity, non-hierarchy and openness. He also made it clear that letting others undertake tasks often only left to professionals – curating from a gallery's collection, for example – can provide enriching experiences for both participants and public. I think I can dare to say that what he has enabled us to achieve as an institution over the last six months of planning and implementing *The Sound We Make Together (Melbourne)* is unprecedented in the NGV's history. In fact, it might be unprecedented throughout the playing field of large encyclopaedic art galleries in general. Thanks to Harrell Fletcher for providing the NGV with this most rewarding experience.

Finally, a word of thanks to all at the NGV who supported and worked so hard on *The Sound We Make Together (Melbourne)*. I want to thank Gerard Vaughan, Director, and Frances Lindsay, Deputy Director, who believed in my idea of a Harrell Fletcher project upon presenting it to them soon after my arrival from the United States. The staff at NGV was incredibly open and supportive every step of the way during planning and facilitation. In particular, I want to thank Garry Sommerfeld, Manager, Photographic Services, and members of his team: Philip White, Justine Frost and Selina Ou; Jean-Pierre Chabrol, Head of Multimedia, and members of his team: Leon Van De Graff, Matt Lim, Tim Hoffman and Steven Phillips; Nicole Monteiro, Exhibitions Manager, and Cherie McNair, Senior Exhibitions Coordinator; Johanna Kelly, Exhibition Designer; Ross Taylor and Adam Pyett, Art Handlers; Allison O'Connell, Associate Registrar; Garth McLean, Senior Technical Assistant; Catherine Earley, Senior Conservator; Eamon O'Toole, Conservation Technician; Emma Mayall, Acting Curator, and Jane Devery, Assistant Curator, in the department of Contemporary Art; Judith Ryan, Senior Curator, and Stephen Gilchrist, Curator, in the department of Indigenous Art; and Robyn Dold, Senior Program Coordinator.

Alex Baker
Senior Curator, Contemporary Art

Harrell Fletcher (born 1967) has worked collaboratively and individually on a variety of socially engaged, interdisciplinary projects for over fifteen years. His work has been shown at San Francisco Museum of Modern Art, De Young Museum, Berkeley Art Museum and Yerba Buena Center for the Arts, all in the San Francisco Bay Area; the Drawing Center, Socrates Sculpture Park, the Sculpture Center, Wrong Gallery, Apex Art and Smackmellon, all in New York; DiverseWorks and Aurora Picture Show, both in Houston, Texas; Portland Institute of Contemporary Art, Portland, Oregon; Seattle Art Museum, Seattle, Washington; Signal, Malmö, Sweden; Domain de Kerguéhennec , Brittany, France; Royal College of Art, London; and Power Plant, Toronto, among others. He was included in the 2004 Whitney Biennial. Fletcher has work in the collections of the Museum of Modern Art, Whitney Museum, New Museum, San Francisco Museum of Modern Art, Berkeley Art Museum, De Young Museum and FRAC, Brittany, France. In 2002 Fletcher started *Learning to Love You More* (LTLYM) with Miranda July, an ongoing participatory website that accepted its final upload in 2009. A book version of LTLYM was published in 2007 by Prestel. Fletcher is the 2005 recipient of the Alpert Award in Visual Arts. His exhibition *The American War* originated in 2005 at ArtPace, San Antonio, Texas and travelled to Solvent Space, Richmond, Virginia; White Columns, New York; the Center for Advanced Visual Studies, Massachusetts Institute of Technology, Boston; and LAXART, Los Angeles, among other venues. *The People's Biennal*, co-curated with Jens Hoffman, director of the CCA Wattis Institute for Contemporary Arts, San Francisco, opens in September 2010 and tours to five American cities. Fletcher is a Professor of Art and Social Practice at Portland State University in Portland, Oregon.

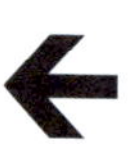

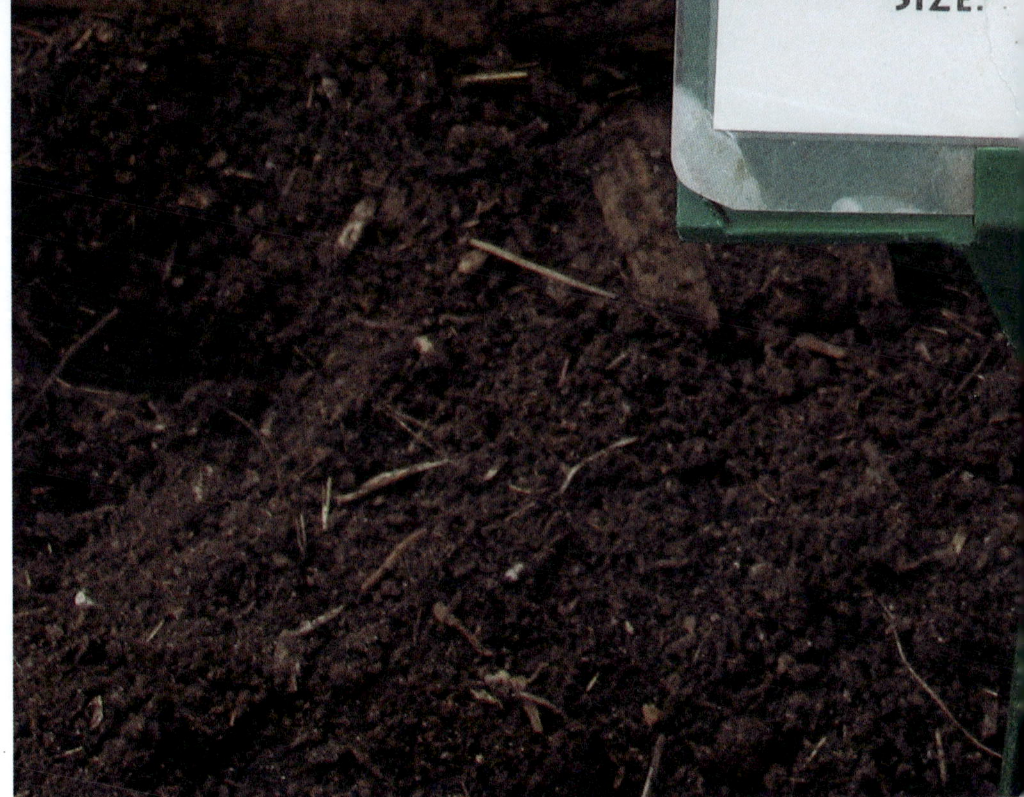

HARRELL FLETCHER

THE SOUND WE MAKE TOGETHER (MELBOURNE)

CERES (Centre for Education and Research in Environmental Strategies) is an internationally recognised model of a sustainable society located in East Brunswick, a suburb of Melbourne. CERES runs on renewable energy, it conserves and recycles its water and waste, grows organic food and teaches diverse audiences about environmentally friendly ways of living. What makes the CERES concept particularly compelling is that sustainability initiatives are located in a participatory social setting which, over time, has created a village-like environment. CERES is renowned for its farmers' market, bicycle repair program and organic outdoor cafe, among many other offerings, and has ben operating for nearly thirty years.

CERES

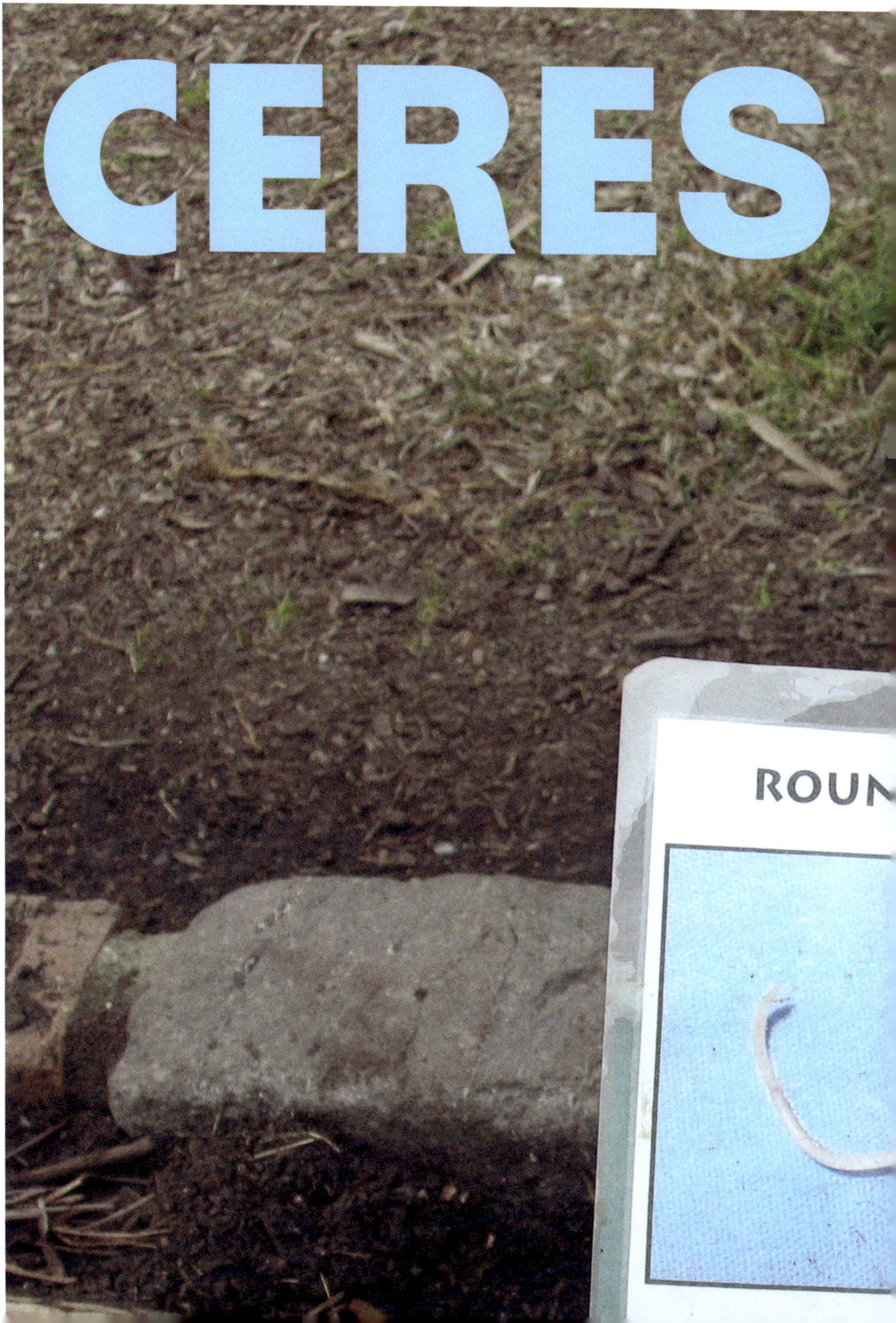

ROUN

People often ask how I'm able to entice random strangers into working with me. The answer is that I appear to actually be interested in the person and his or her activities. And what is the best strategy for appearing interested? The answer is sincerely be interested; in fact nothing else will work. This is not difficult for me, because I think that people are interesting. I would even go so far as to say that I have a great fondness for the human race.[1]

Harrell Fletcher

Harrell Fletcher is internationally renowned for facilitating exhibitions and events based on participation and collaboration, often with people who are not involved in making art. From a temporary museum in a California shopping mall focusing on local people's lives to working with an eight-year-old boy on a work of public art for a park in Brittany to helping realise the aesthetic aspirations of a petrol station owner, Fletcher provides a means for others to present who they are and what they do.

Fletcher spent a week in Melbourne during March 2010 to meet potential participants for his project at National Gallery of Victoria. Over the course of the following two months, Fletcher and I had an email exchange regarding who we would invite and what the parameters of the project might be. Despite Fletcher's collaborative generosity, he admits that there is a self-interested aspect to what he does: to learn more about a particular place where he will be working; in this instance, Melbourne and the NGV.

The participants each reveal an aspect of contemporary and historical Melbourne, whether it is immigration, art and community, identity, urban agriculture and sustainability, urban history and politics or even music. In addition to reflecting a place's past and present, the project is ultimately situated in an art gallery and Fletcher saw this as an opportunity to involve participants in selecting works from the NGV collection as a central component. Fletcher decided that *The Sound We Make Together (Melbourne)* would combine three basic elements: an installation of NGV works of art selected by the participants juxtaposed with photographs taken by Fletcher during his August 2010 residency; presentations and performances featuring the participants and their invited guests (video-taped and presented in the gallery context as a document of the weekend of events); a representation of each participant through reading materials and printed ephemera (newsletters, books, posters); objects or works of art that affirm something about each would also be included. In addition to this very site-specific endeavour, I thought it important to give our audience some insight into the art of Harrell Fletcher which, when it does venture into the realm of things and images – his work just as often does not – takes on the form of more humble modes of expression: posters, self-published booklets (zines) and video.

Until quite recently the contemporary art world had been fixated on the notion of the artist as object-making superstar and the glamour associated with art fairs, international biennials and mind-boggling

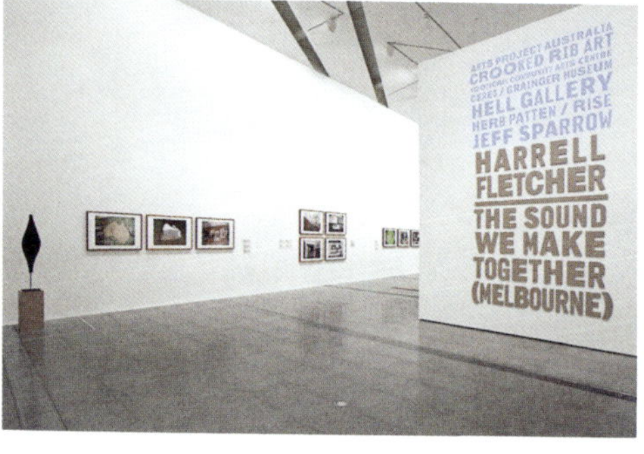

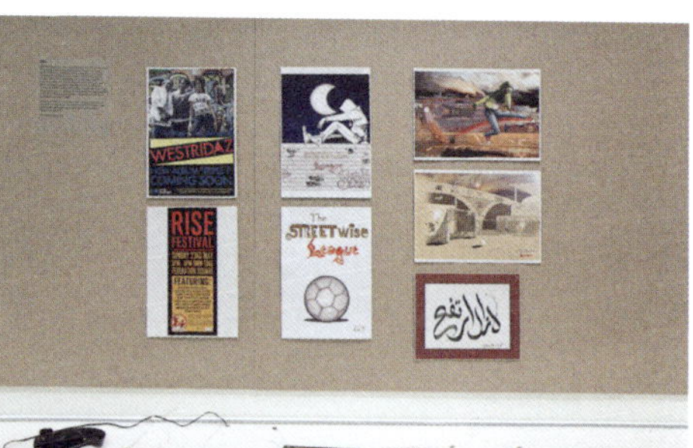

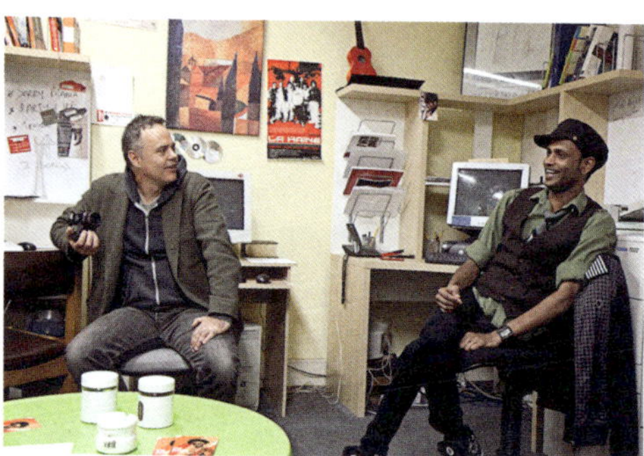
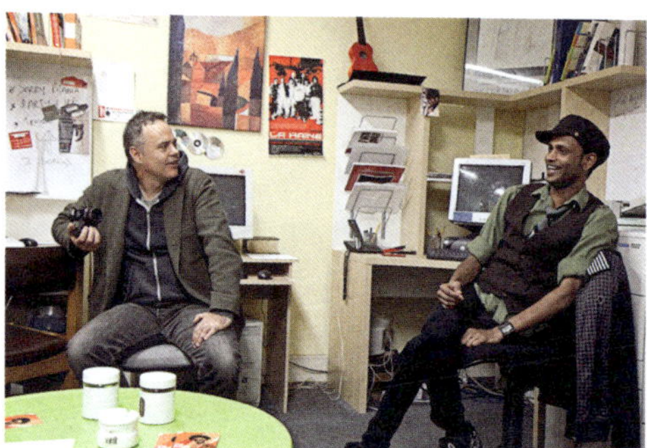

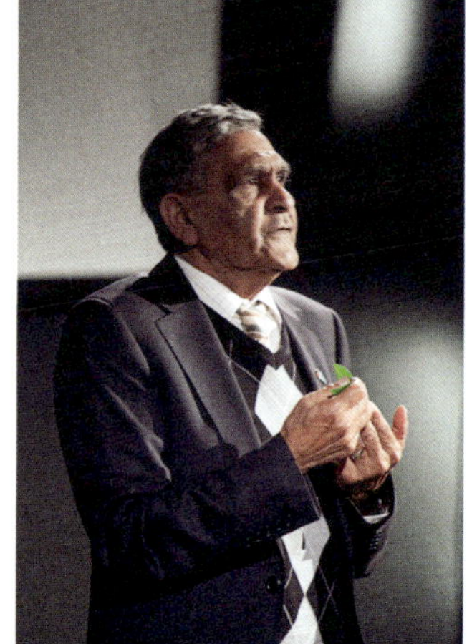

clockwise from upper left:

The Sound We Make Together (Melbourne), installation view
Unknown, *Broad shield* (19th century)
selected from NGV collection
by Herb Patten with Harrell
Fletcher photographs

The Sound We Make Together (Melbourne), installation detail
RISE posters, ephemera,
listening station

Herb Patten performing on
14 August 2010

Harrell Fletcher (left) and Ramesh
Fernandez (right), RISE office

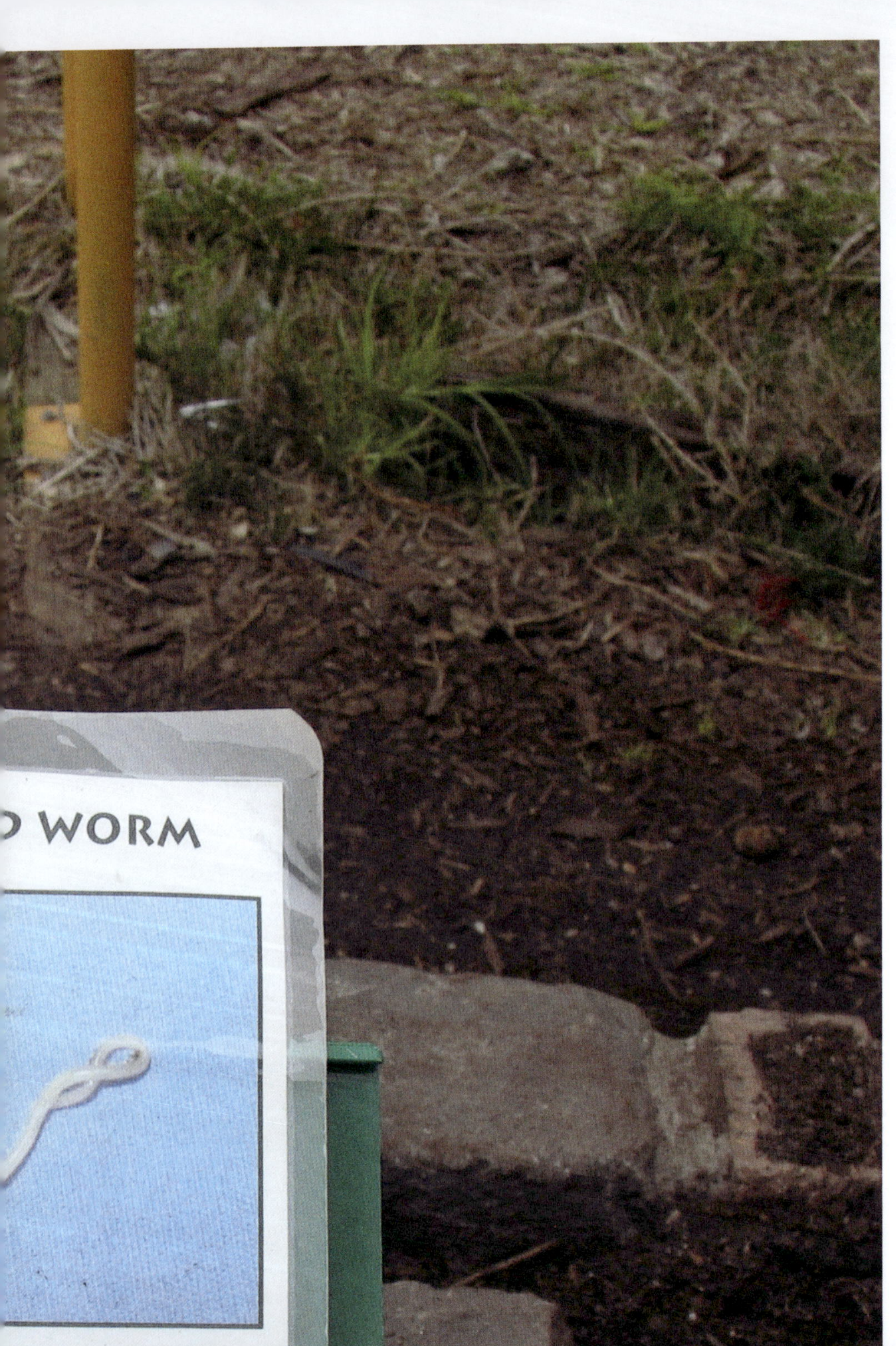
WORM

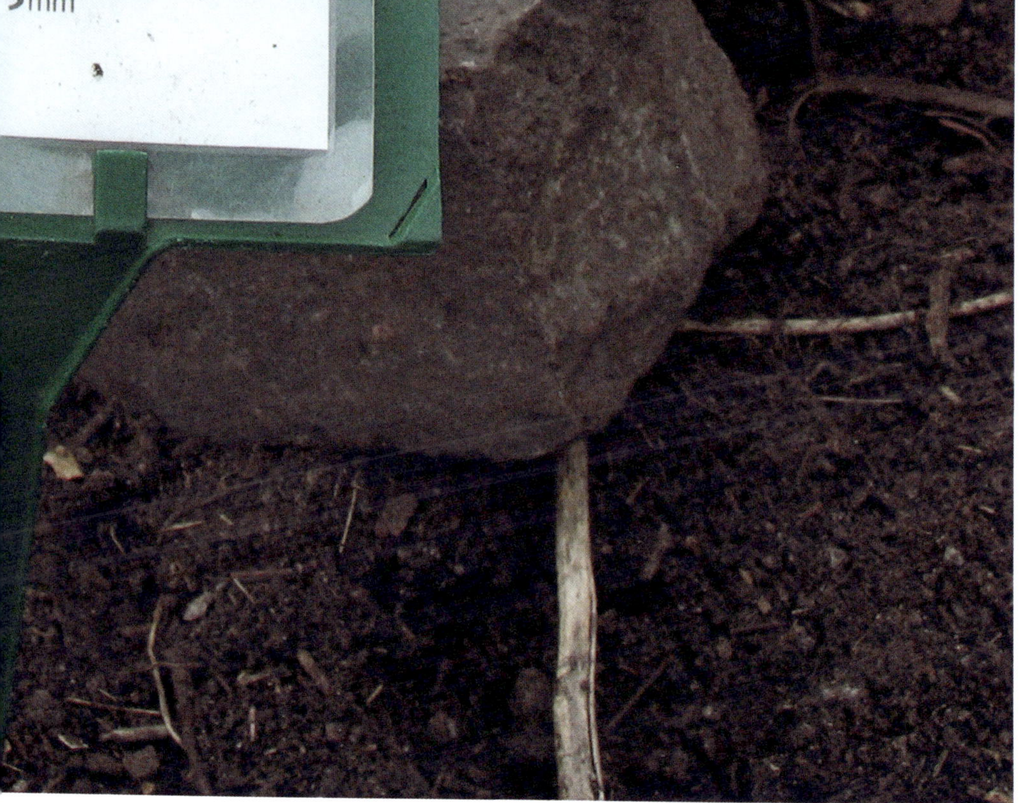

11 SEP – 30 JAN 11

CERES
Corner Roberts and Stewart Streets
Brunswick East Victoria 3057
www.ceres.org.au

Harrell Fletcher
Round worm marker, CERES 2010 (detail)
colour inkjet print
Collection of the artist,
Portland, Oregon

ngv
National Gallery of Victoria

auction figures. Then the global financial crisis dampened the party. Harrell Fletcher affirms another way of being an artist that resonates within the context of our leaner, less ostentatious time. In a practice spanning fifteen years, Fletcher makes few sellable objects, shuns the well-heeled collector circuit and eschews the cult of personality so often associated these days with artists. Fletcher directs the spotlight away from himself by shifting attention onto the aspirations and talents of others. His practice, despite its marked contrast to much recent contemporary art, is not without context or precedent. It draws on the instructional art of the 1960s and 1970s including Fluxus, Conceptual art and feminist art movements, 1990s American community art known as 'New Genre Public Art',[2] and recent forms of contemporary art categorised as 'relational aesthetics' or art whose meaning is generated by the social context of human interaction.[3]

The Sound We Make Together (Melbourne) at the NGV can also be situated within institutional critique, contemporary art which uses the museum and gallery as the site and subject of its investigation (institutionally critical practices include artists posing as tour guides; artists working as curators and engaging with museum collections; and artists' architectural, archival and historical explorations of the museum, among a range of other possibilities). However, Fletcher's institutional engagement is less about heavy-handed critique and more invested in simply providing people with a unique platform. By offering Melbourne community groups, organisations and individuals a curatorial role in the project as both selectors of NGV works of art

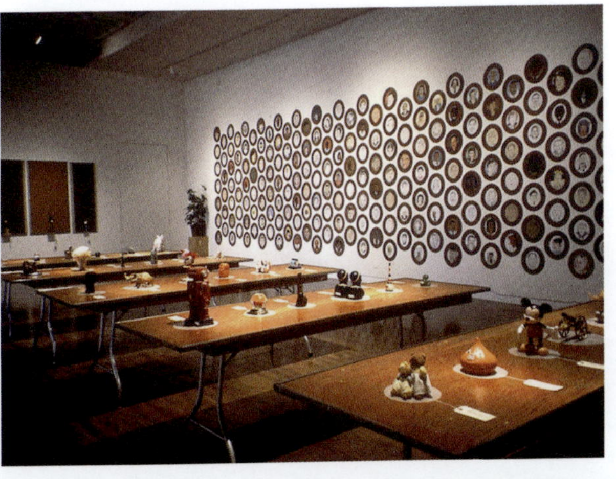

Harrell Fletcher and Jon Rubin
Some People We Met 1996,
installation view
Richmond Arts Center,
Richmond, California

and lenders of their own materials and objects to the NGV, Fletcher provides access into the professionalised realm of the art world. This is a sphere that members of the public are rarely, if ever, privy to and Fletcher's gesture suggests a transformation of the art museum from temple to forum and a discourse shift from monologue to dialogue.[4]

As much as Fletcher focuses on fostering relationships among participants, his practice also centres on things, even if he rarely makes them himself. Fletcher is deeply invested in how we create our symbolic universe from the stuff that surrounds us. While often shunning the making of objects for sale in commercial galleries, he remains highly attuned to the fact that objects define our humanness. For a project realised during his graduate school years, *Gallery HERE*, 1993–95, Fletcher and collaborator Jon Rubin borrowed a vacant building in which they presented exhibitions about people and places in the neighbourhood; once again, examining the material culture that defines personhood. One exhibition focused on the rugs that a local rug merchant sold across the street. In another, the artists asked neighbourhood people to have a garage sale in the gallery and each object had an interpretive tag explaining the relevance of the item to its owner. Still others focused on a local man's courtyard garden or the burritos that were available in the neighbourhood. In *Some People We Met*, 1996, municipal employees volunteered to display their favourite knick-knacks, personal photographs and plants from their workplaces, highlighting how people individualise their mundane environments with personal belongings. In *Maintaining the jazz*, 2004 (on view in this exhibition as a component of Fletcher's existing work, see pp.24–25), Fletcher photographed various objects on display in artist Shaun O'Dell's home. He then created a series of posters combining the photographs of O'Dell's world of objects with comments by the artist about something else that was meaningful – his drawings.

The Sound We Make Together (Melbourne) similarly explores participants' identities through objects and calls into question distinctions often made between art and more humble items. An office filing cabinet, a scrapbook or a festival banner displayed in close proximity to works of art from the NGV collection reveal a levelling process at work in Fletcher's practice. Barriers and distinctions made between so-called high and low culture are ultimately irrelevant as resonant meaning can be generated from objects of any kind, from any place and from any culture. When Fletcher mounted *Some People We Met* in 1996 – the exhibition of municipal employees' favourite

Notes

1 'Towards a tender society', 2002, online at <www.harrellfletcher.com>, viewed August 2010

2 See Suzanne Lacy (ed.), *Mapping the Terrain: New Genre Public Art*, Bay Press, Seattle, 1995. This text explores the range of practices in early 1990s American contemporary art addressing identity politics and multiculturalism, specifically the shift in public art from sculptures in space to public art as a more process-oriented form of audience engagement.

3 See Nicolas Bourriaud, *Relational Aesthetics* [1998], trans. Simon Pleasance & Fronza Woods, Les Presses du Réel, Dijon, 2002.

4 Just as there has been renewed interest in community and participatory art practices within the field of contemporary art, art museums are also returning to notions of participation as integral to both programming and structure. Part of this is fuelled by the realisation that younger people shun the idea of the passive audience and demand participation, hence the embrace of social media, podcasting and digital outreach in general by these institutions. In terms of the art museum's current adoption of participation and audience engagement beyond an enthusiasm for Twitter and Facebook, there are several new developments. Although artists who work in a socially engaged/participatory framework have existed for decades, an increasing enthusiasm for what might be termed the 'social practice' genre by institutions is a definite trend. These are not one-off performances but new structures/departments. In Los Angeles the Hammer Museum recently launched its Public Engagement residency; the Los Angeles County Museum of Art has started LACMA Lab, an educational/curatorial hybrid; and the Museum of Contemporary Art, Los Angeles, recently started its Engagement Party series. In London the Serpentine Gallery has also started a project series dedicated to participatory art making.

HARRELL FLETCHER

THE SOUND WE MAKE TOGETHER (MELBOURNE)

Crooked Rib Art is an art collective started by young Muslim female artists who not only aim to challenge perceptions of themselves but also question perceptions of current social issues through the public art domain. Crooked Rib Art views art as a form of public engagement and as a vehicle for both education and social change. While each artist has their own individual practice, they have worked collaboratively in the design and implementation of several public murals, as well as gallery exhibitions. Recently Crooked Rib Art produced a community centre mural in collaboration with City of Yarra Youth Services and held an exhibition at Desypher Gallery, Fitzroy.

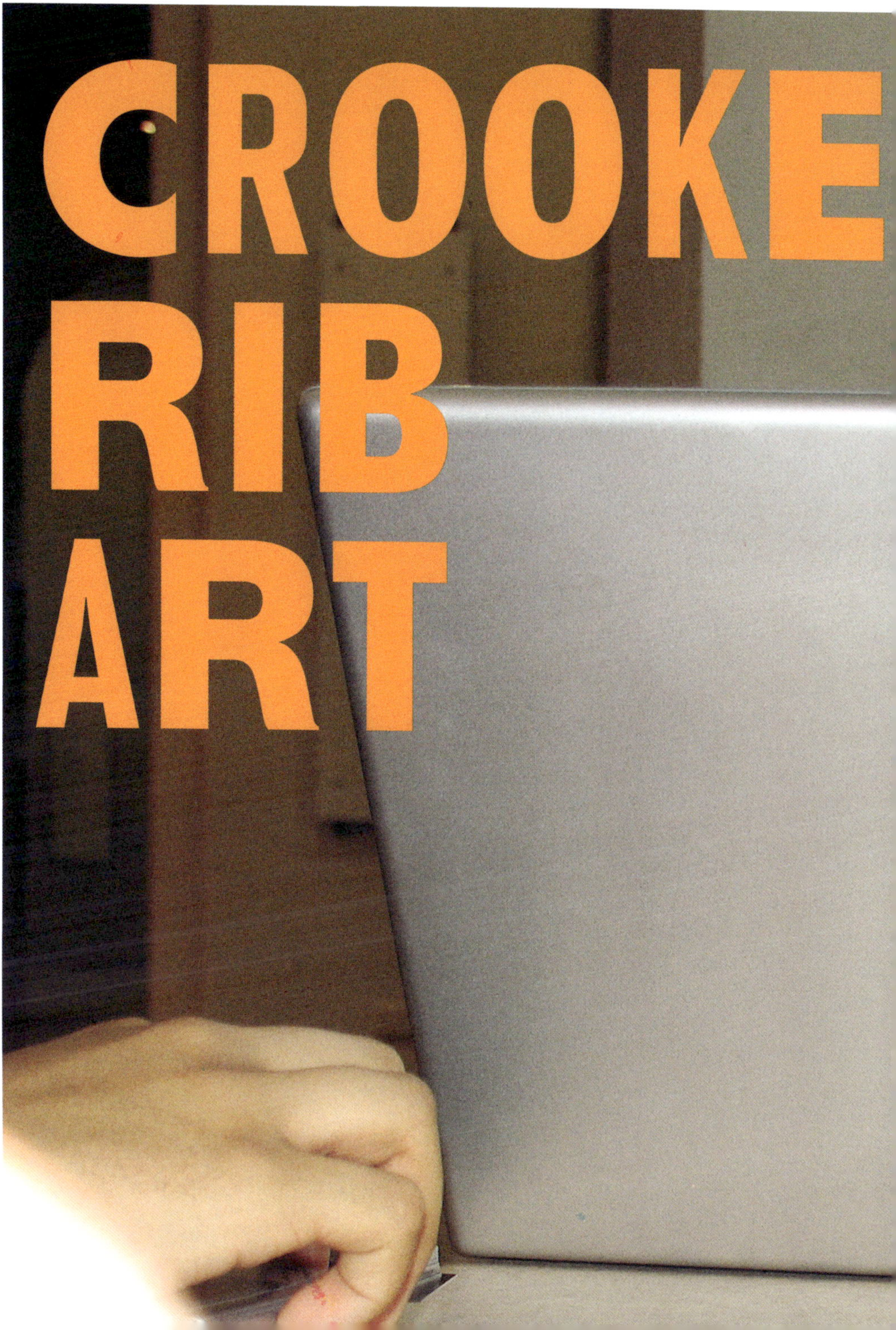

CROOKE
RIB
ART

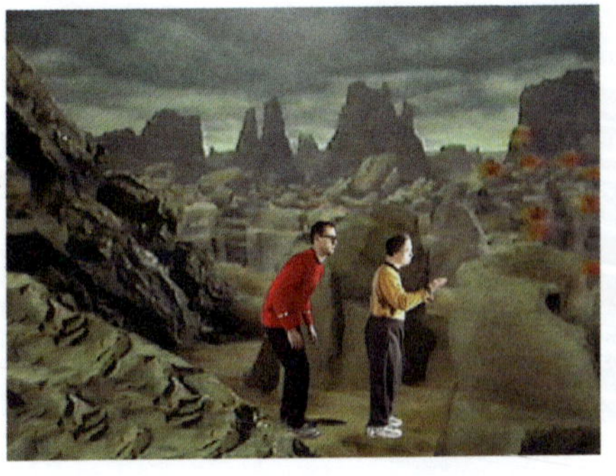

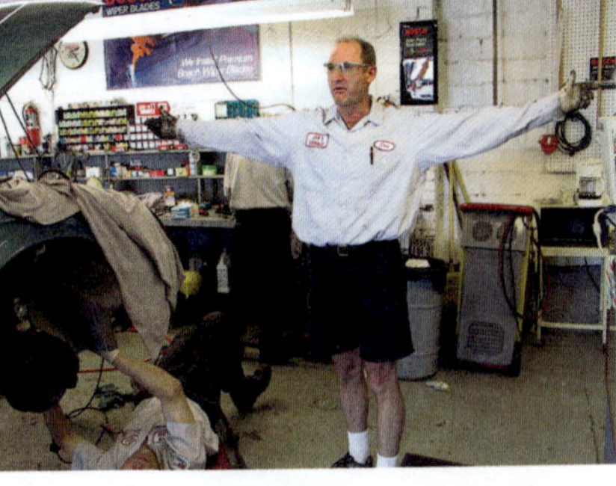

left:
Harrell Fletcher, David Jarvey, Chris Johanson, Elizabeth Meyer and Alexis Van Hurkman
The forbidden zone 2000 (video still)
colour video transferred to DVD, sound, 12 min 46 sec
Collection of the artist, Portland, Oregon

right:
Harrell Fletcher
Blot out the sun 2002 (video still)
colour video transferred to DVD, sound, 22 min 13 sec
Collection of the artist, Portland, Oregon

objects – he did so to make the contemporary art centre, located in the same building that housed civic administration offices, relevant to employees who often felt no ownership toward the art on view. *The Sound We Make Together (Melbourne)* is another example of Fletcher's belief in providing participants with a sense of ownership within the official houses of culture.

Working with me in my role as senior curator of contemporary art, each participant was lead through the daunting but enriching task of visiting the NGV's vast offsite storage facility and choosing a selection of works, one of which would be placed on view. This integral aspect of the exhibition was suggested by Fletcher and the notion that this would be an exercise necessary to the success of the project is firmly situated within what the artist calls 'participatory research', which he teaches in his Art and Social Practice program at Portland State University. In essence it is a kind of ethnography, a form of participant observation within a given activity or situation where the goal is hands-on, self-actualised learning.

In addition to the selection process, each participant was asked to write a brief statement about why the chosen work was appealing or how it represented their organisation – the texts would be used as interpretive wall labels in the gallery space. Each was ascribed authorship by the individual or the selecting organisation, personalising what are often omniscient, authoritative monologues; seemingly authorless texts presented within the museum environment. In another instance of providing a voice within the exhibition context, a video recording of the weekend of performances and presentations involving the nine groups and individuals and several invited guests plays continuously in the gallery space. This constant stream of presentations is situated in the same gallery where works of art, posters, reading material and ephemera on loan from the participants are displayed. The video is another example in which the interests and identities of those involved are underscored in the exhibition – again, in their own words.

Inviting people who, for the most part, have little or no curatorial expertise in determining what hangs on an art museum's walls, privileges those who do not register within the specialised discipline of museum discourse – amateurs.[5] Empowering and collaborating with amateurs, whether they be actors, curators, directors or artists, is an ongoing theme in the art of Harrell Fletcher. David Jarvey, who has Down's syndrome, conceived of and stars in Fletcher's video *The forbidden zone*, 2000, on view in this exhibition. Jay Dykman, the owner of an automotive garage and petrol station in Portland, Oregon, played a significant conceptual role in the Fletcher video *Blot out the sun*, 2002, which also featured amateur actors (also included in the exhibition). Service station employees, customers and local residents together conveyed narratives based on James Joyce's *Ulysses*, reading selected texts from cue cards (Dykman suggested to Fletcher the video should be loosely based on the Joyce novel). Similarly, Fletcher worked with the residents of a senior citizens centre as the non-professional stars in another video based on *Ulysses* titled *The problem of possible redemption*, 2003, also featured in the NGV exhibition. When Fletcher needed portraits of civic centre employees for the exhibition *Some People We Met* he enlisted local schoolchildren and senior citizens to paint portraits based on photographs that Fletcher took of his subjects. Corentine Senechal, an eight-year-old boy with no experience as a sculptor or in the complex world of public art, designed a public sculpture of a turtle for a park in Brittany for Fletcher's project, *Corentine's turtle*, 2003. Fletcher and a team of professionals mentored the boy through every phase from art historical context to fabrication to installation. Fletcher has even assisted marginalised non-professional artists with their careers. In one instance Michael Patterson-Carver, an artist living and selling his work on the streets of Portland, Oregon, found representation in New York and European commercial art galleries with Fletcher's aid. *Learning To Love You More*, 2002–2009, a website collaboration with Miranda July, was premised on the participation of anyone who wished to take up the assignments offered on the site. The project is essentially a virtual art gallery for amateur artists, albeit one with parameters to follow.

Notes

5 For an interesting exploration of the amateur in contemporary art, see Ralph Rugoff, *Amateurs*, CCA Wattis Institute of Contemporary Arts, San Francisco, 2008. Rugoff argues that the idea of the amateur resonates on several levels in contemporary culture. For example, the internet, a forum for amateur filmmakers and photographers with sites such as YouTube and Flickr; amateur critics, historians and an infinite number of other knowledge categories as demonstrated in sites such as Wikipedia. There are blogs which sliver and splinter human enthusiasms and endeavours into even more specialised fields of knowledge (or pedantry). Within the field of contemporary art there has been a backlash against the hyper-professionalism within the art world, both in terms of the production values within art-making itself and the infrastructures of distribution and presentation. The embrace ranges from artists working with amateur collaborators and participants to documentations of existing amateur cultural productions to art that borrows from amateur aesthetics and forms of creation.

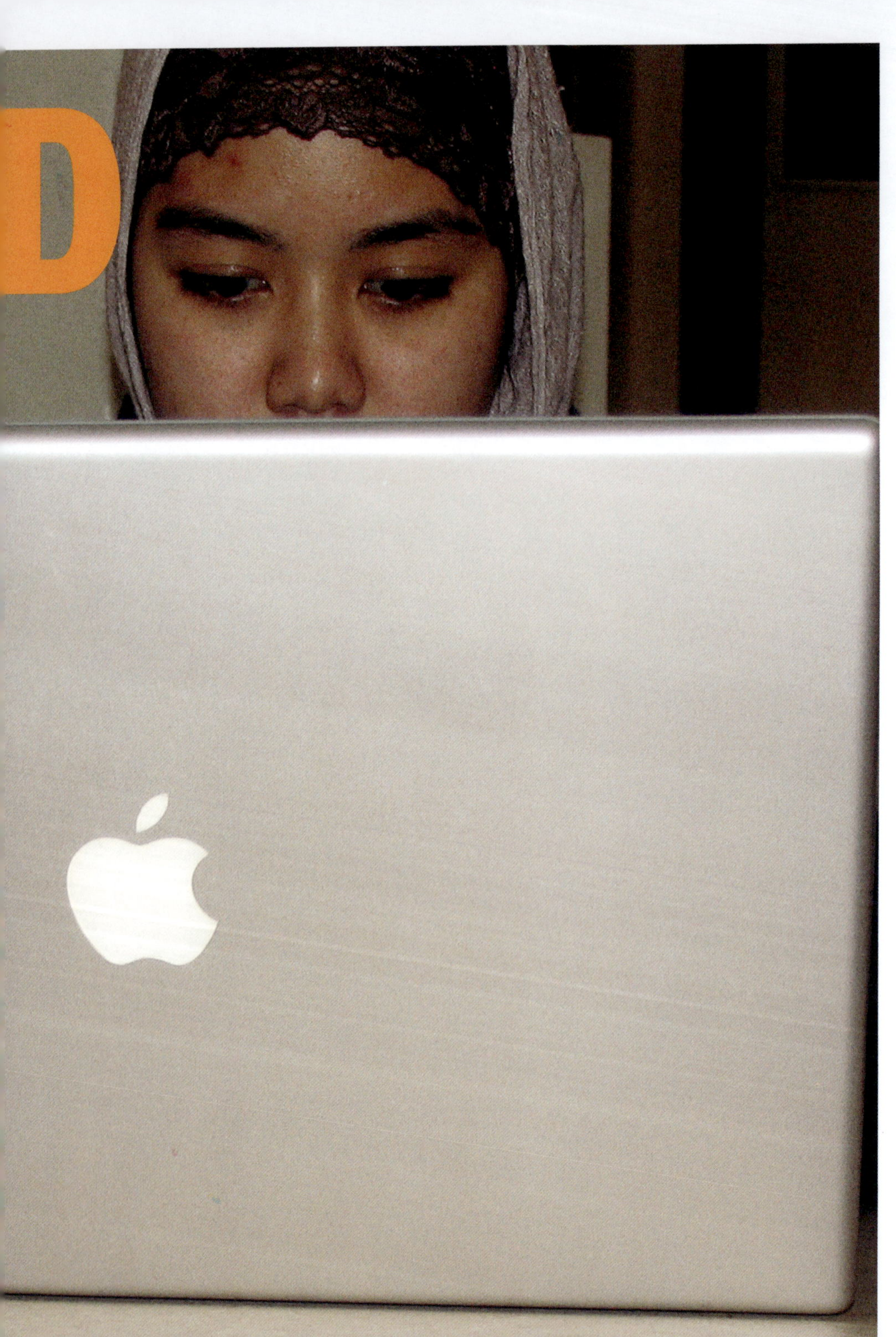

11 SEP -
30 JAN 11

Crooked Rib Art
www.crookedribart.com

Harrell Fletcher
Pesuri Ahmad, Crooked Rib Art meeting, State Library of Victoria 2010 (detail)
colour inkjet print
Collection of the artist,
Portland, Oregon

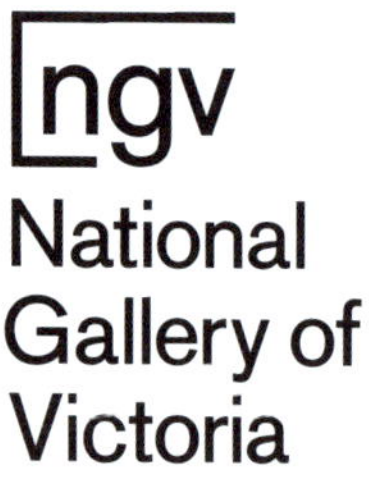

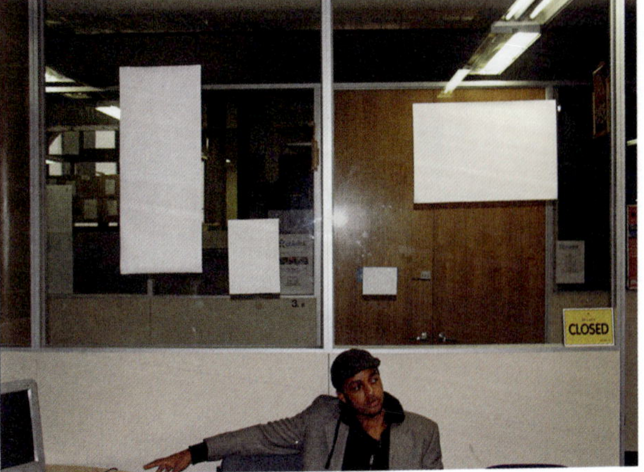

Harrell Fletcher
Frank Mwamba, RISE office 2010
colour inkjet print
Collection of the artist,
Portland, Oregon

Fletcher's photographs included in *The Sound We Make Together (Melbourne)* that are juxtaposed with NGV works in the main gallery were taken during a week in August leading up to the opening of the exhibition. During this time Fletcher and I visited the participants in their workplaces or other sites of significance. The visits resembled a form of anthropological fieldwork in which information was elicited through informal conversation. Dialogue was supplemented by another tool from the anthropologist's kit, the camera, which Fletcher used to document the physical contexts of the various sites. He admits that these images do not in any way attempt social scientific objectivity; on the contrary, they represent 'my aesthetic sensibility, which has been developing in regards to photography since I was a child'.[6] The photographs build on Fletcher's continued interest in how people 'curate their lives through posters they put up in their offices, their collections of books and objects that accumulate on shelves and tables'.[7] Mostly the photographs focus not so much on people but on how people physically and materially create their worlds. In some cases the worlds that Fletcher has chosen to depict are more formally constructed (for example, displays photographed at the Aboriginal Advancement League or at CERES);[8] in other photographs the artwork or material culture is decidedly behind the scenes (such as the storage facilities at Arts Project Australia and the Grainger Museum or the archives at Jeff Sparrow's *Overland* office); and elsewhere Fletcher has chosen to document posters on office walls or windows – these are more akin to public expressions of the self or group. He notes that there is an underlying resonance between the selection exercise undertaken by the participants and the photographic component of the exhibition:

> The photographs are intended to give viewers a sense of the places where the participants come from, while being paired with their selections of objects from the NGV collection – the participants were invited to NGV storage and made selections based on what was available and what they were interested in. I have done a similar thing in their work places and cultural locations.[9]

Connections can be made across the different exhibition components of *The Sound We Make Together (Melbourne)*. Fletcher's emphasis on the participants' physical and object-related environments resonates with items on loan from the respective organisations and individuals: items such as newsletters, posters and books that are displayed in the exhibition are just as likely to find themselves the subject of Fletcher's photographs in an adjacent gallery. Aside from photography, when Fletcher does elect to create art with a material presence, he often chooses to work in formats like posters and printed ephemera. *The Sound Me Make Together (Melbourne)* features a selection of this kind of material by Fletcher, revealing again the artist's interest in how more humble modes of expression can speak just as powerfully as more rarefied objects. Synthesising various elements of the project for this publication, Fletcher has worked with Graphic Designer Dirk Hiscock in creating a poster identity for each participant, based on photographs featured in the exhibition.

As this exhibition and other projects discussed here make clear, Fletcher's primary motivation is based on openness to the lives of ordinary people who, as he would be the first to point out, are usually far from ordinary. Implicit in all of Fletcher's work is a subtle upending of the art world, whose tastes can be restrictive and discriminatory, often leaving out the very people that Fletcher seeks to collaborate with and address. Never polemic or overtly critical, Fletcher is not suggesting institutional revolution but a simple opening up of art world structures to other voices and perspectives. As Fletcher is quick to point out, and *The Sound We Make Together (Melbourne)* demonstrates, such voices are always present in our midst. We simply need to attune ourselves to hear them in the first place, or adjust our senses to hear those voices in new ways.

Alex Baker
Senior Curator, Contemporary Art

Notes

6 Harrell Fletcher, 'Site photographs', exhibition wall text, in *The Sound We Make Together (Melbourne)*.

7 ibid. As mentioned earlier in this essay, Fletcher has had a continued interest in how people create meaning in their lives through the things they collect and display in their homes, offices and front yards.

8 Fletcher has a keen interest in how information is officially presented in exhibition contexts and has documented these in the past. In his project *The American War*, 2005, he photographed the displays of an entire museum, the War Remnants Museum in Ho Chi Minh City, Vietnam, an institution devoted to showcasing American atrocities inflicted upon the Vietnamese people during what they refer to as 'The American War'.

9 Fletcher, 'Site photographs'.

Further reading

Baker, Alex. 'It's all about you: Generosity in the art of Harrell Fletcher', *Melbourne Art Journal*, 11–12, 2009, pp. 136–49.
Fletcher, Harrell. *The American War*. J & L Books, Atlanta, Georgia, 2006.
Fletcher, Harrell & Miranda July. *Learning to Love You More*. Prestel, New York, 2008.
Fletcher, Harrell. 'Questionnaire: Fletcher'. *October*, Winter 2008, pp. 49–52.
— *Where I Lived, and What I Lived For*. Domaine de Kerguéhennec, Bignan, France, 2008.
— & Michael Rakowitz. *Between Artists*. Art Resources Transfer Press, New York, 2008.
Hoffman, Jens. 'You and me.' *Frieze*, November–December 2008, pp.192–5.
Miles, James F. with Harrell Fletcher. *Is a Boyfriend and a Girlfriend*. The Expanding Color System/1 Artist 1 Concept, San Francisco, 2007.

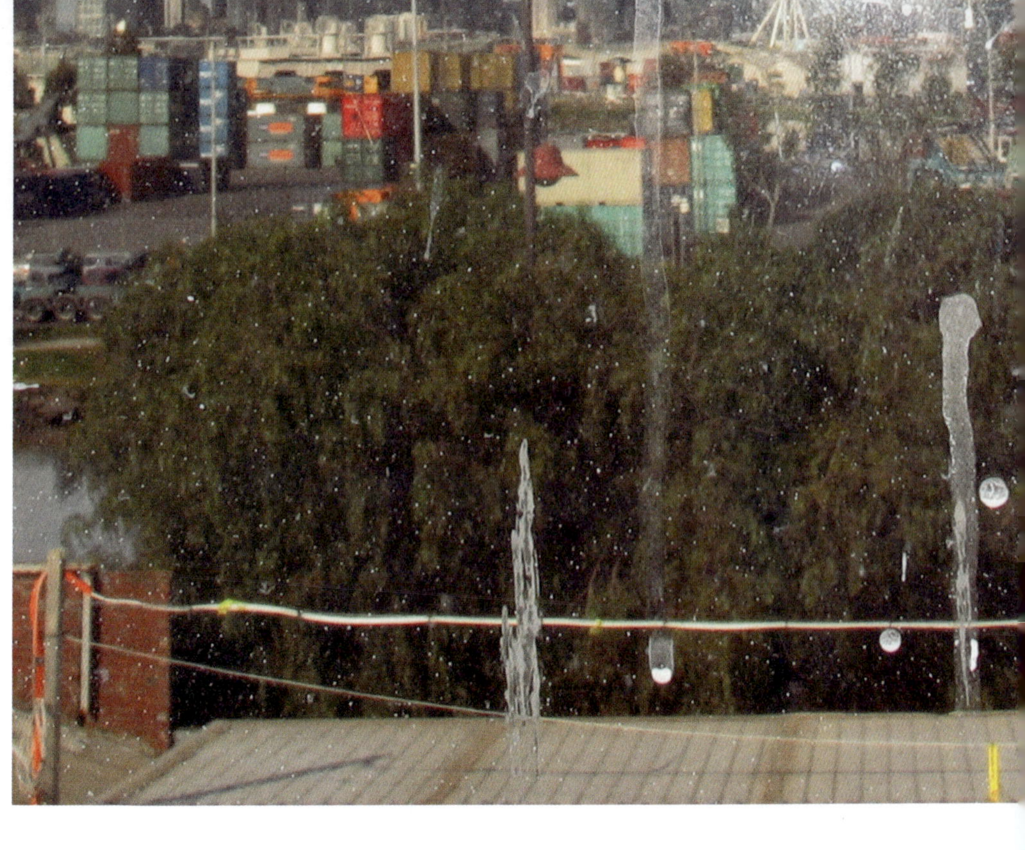

HARRELL FLETCHER

THE SOUND WE MAKE TOGETHER (MELBOURNE)

Since 1974 Footscray Community Arts Centre has been advancing community arts and cultural development practice in Australia. The centre is a vibrant hub of artistic activity for local artists and community groups, as well as for leading artists and cultural-development practitioners. Footscray Community Arts Centre offers the diverse communities of Melbourne's west a venue and an opportunity for cultural expression, participation and exchange. It is a unique place of learning and sharing where the dynamics between community, culture and contemporary art is explored and celebrated. In 2011 a new gallery and performance centre will open, positioning it as the west's leading multi-arts venue.

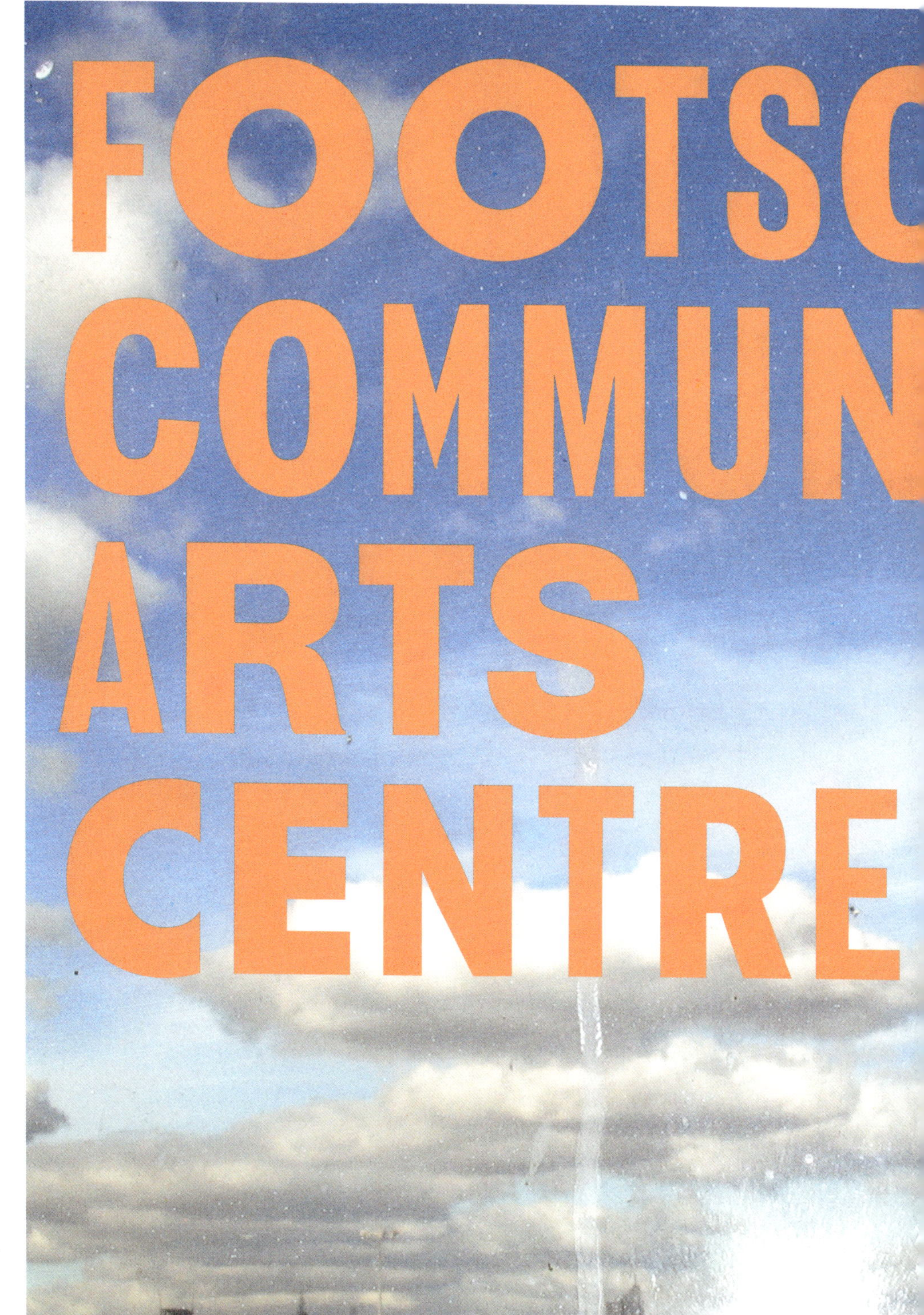
FOOTSC
COMMUN
ARTS
CENTRE

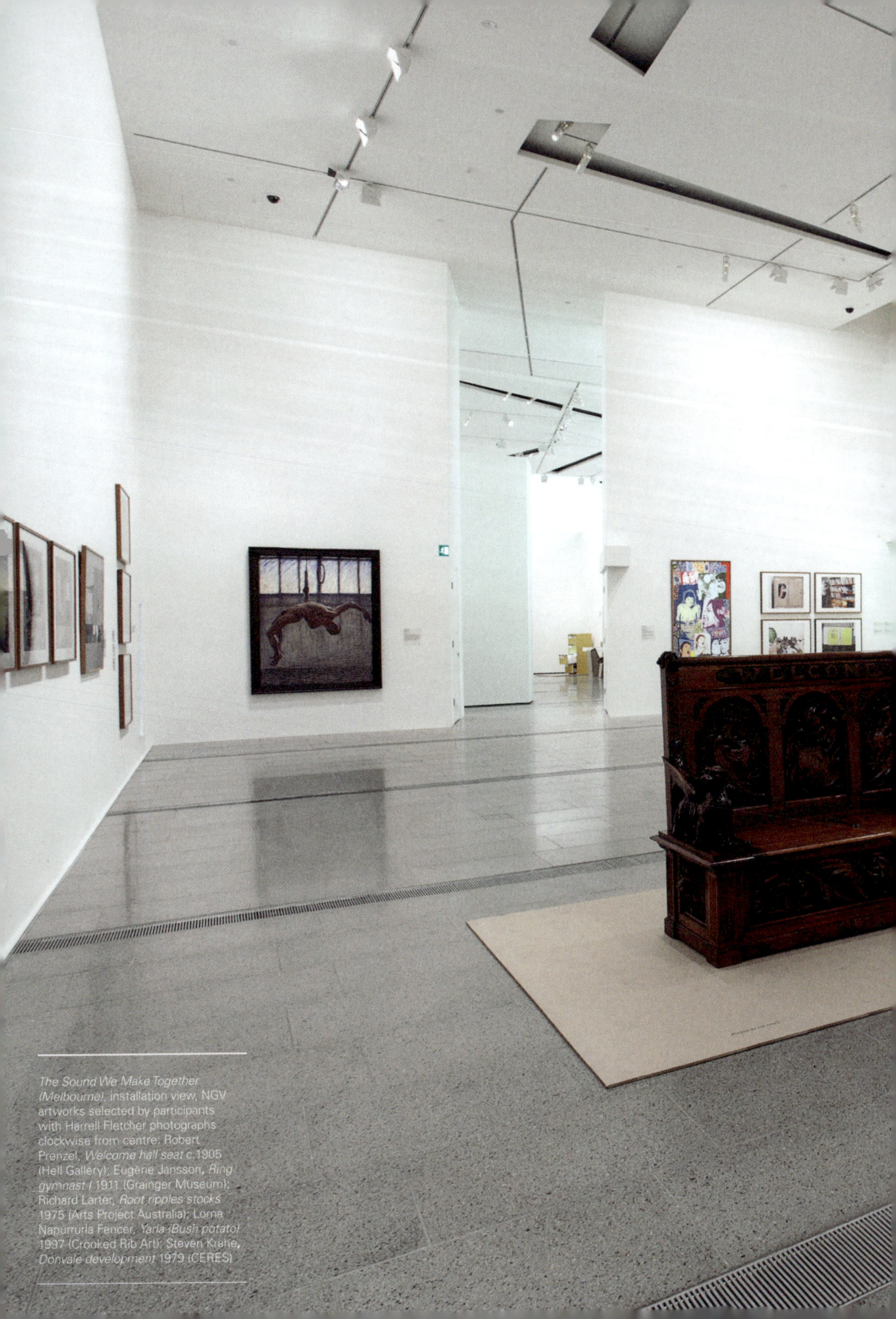

The Sound We Make Together (Melbourne), installation view, NGV artworks selected by participants with Harrell Fletcher photographs clockwise from centre: Robert Prenzel, *Welcome hall seat* c.1905 (Hell Gallery); Eugène Jansson, *Ring gymnast I* 1911 (Grainger Museum); Richard Larter, *Root ripples stocks* 1975 (Arts Project Australia); Lorna Napurrurla Fencer, *Yarla (Bush potato)* 1997 (Crooked Rib Art); Steven Krahe, *Donvale development* 1979 (CERES)

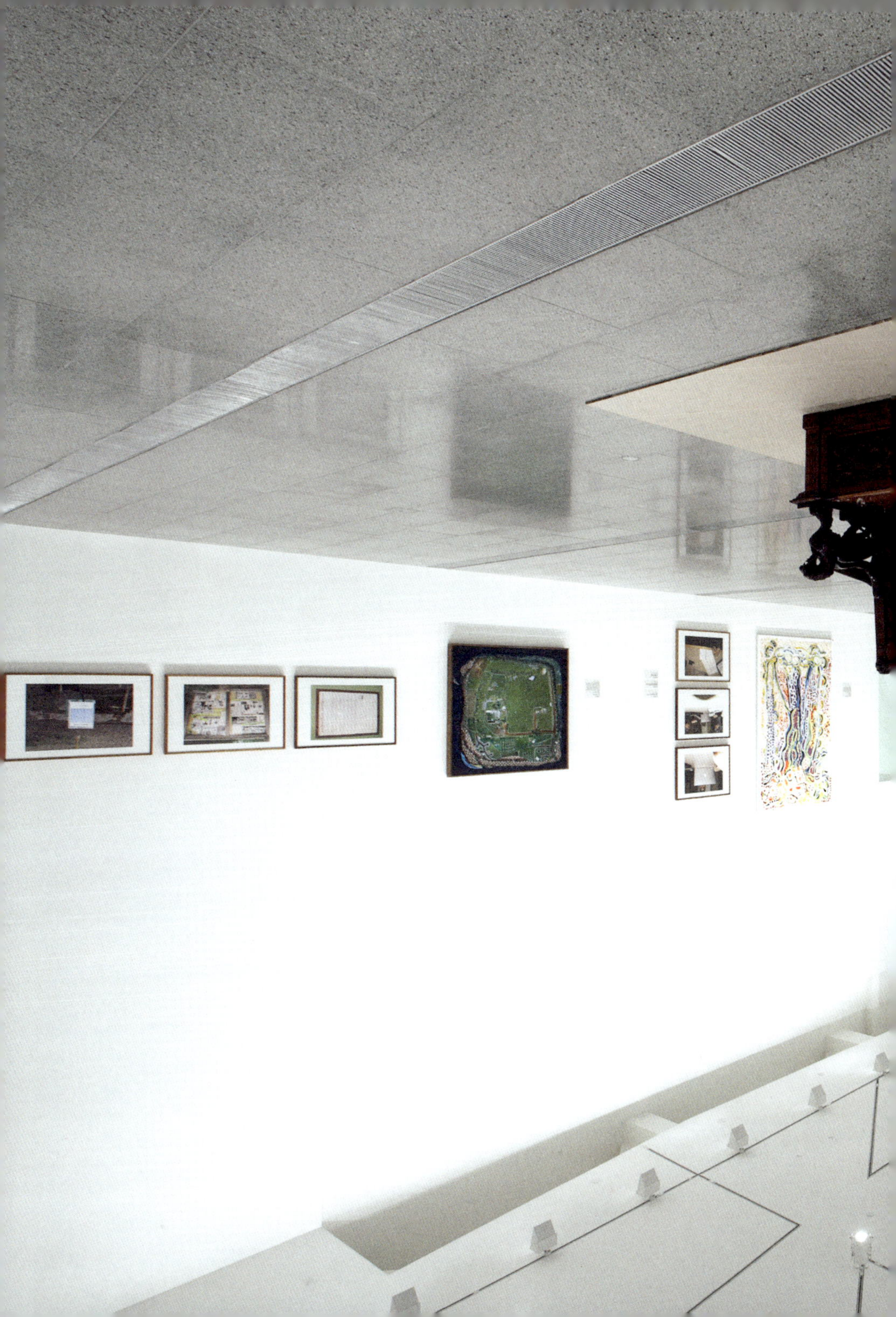

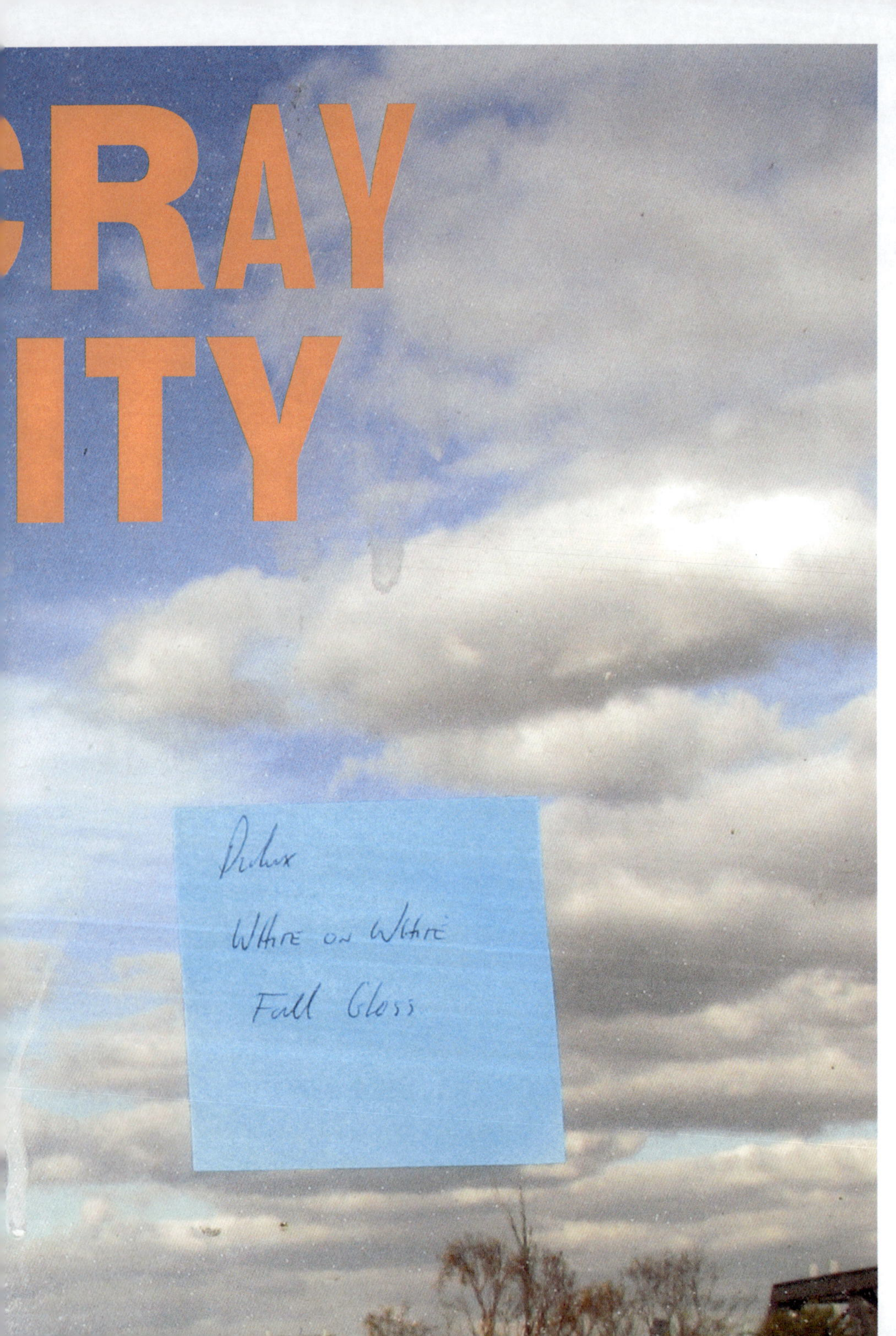
CRAY
ITY
Dulux
White on White
Full Gloss

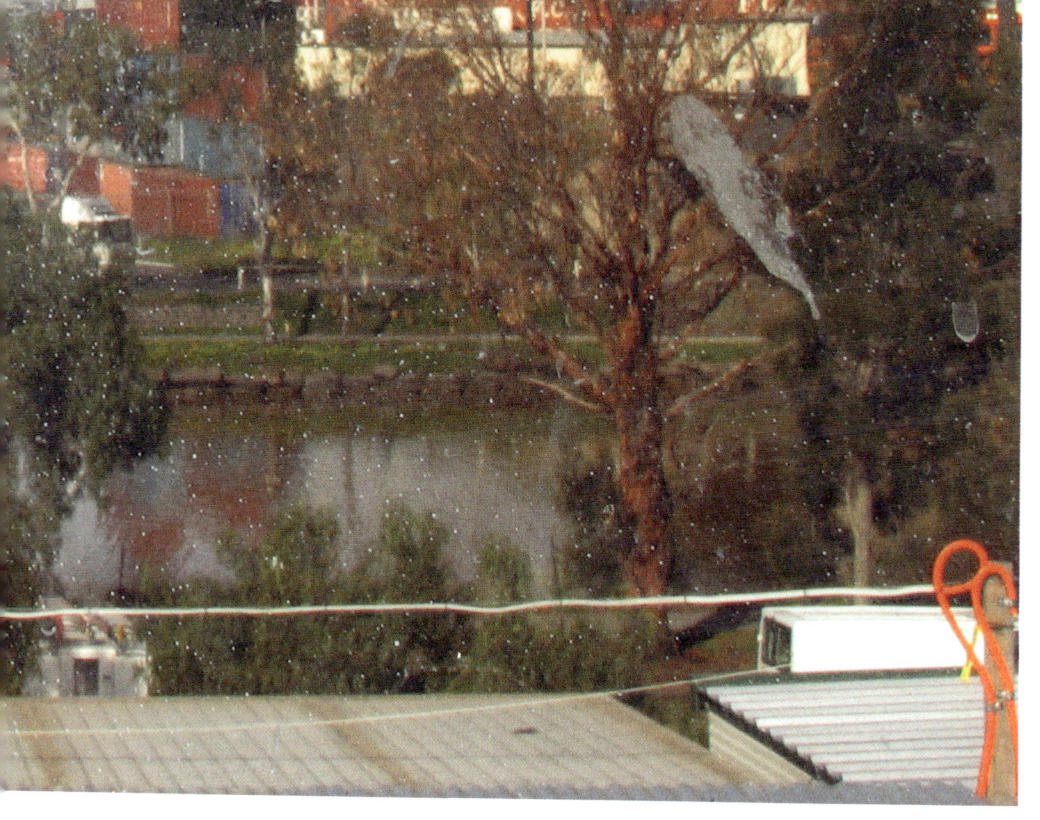

11 SEP -
30 JAN 11

Footscray Community Arts Centre
45 Moreland Street
Footscray Victoria 3011
www.footscrayarts.com

Harrell Fletcher
Window view, new building under construction, Footscray Community Arts Centre 2010 (detail)
colour inkjet print
Collection of the artist,
Portland, Oregon

ngv
National Gallery of Victoria

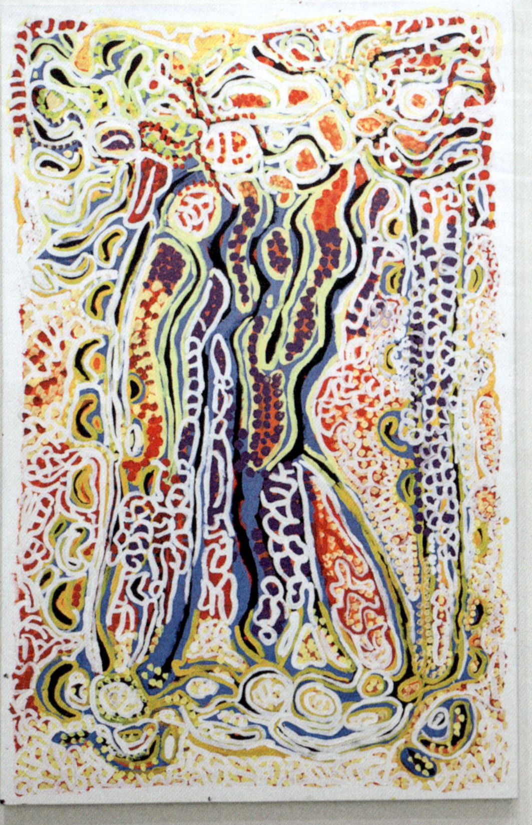

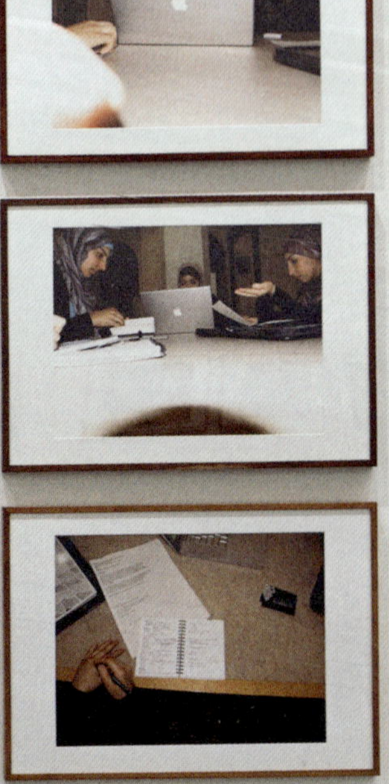

left:
Lorna Napurrurla Fencer (Yulyulu)
Warlpiri (c. 1925) –2006
Yarla (Bush potato) 1997
synthetic polymer paint on canvas
National Gallery of Victoria, Melbourne
Purchased through The Art
Foundation of Victoria with the
assistance of Mobil Oil Australia
Limited, Fellow, 1998
Selected by Crooked Rib Art right,

top to bottom:
Harrell Fletcher
Crooked Rib Art Meeting, State Library of Victoria 2010
colour inkjet print
Collection of the artist,
Portland, Oregon

opposite:
top left:
Richard Larter
born England 1929,
arrived Australia 1962
Root ripples stocks 1975
synthetic polymer paint on
canvas on composition board
National Gallery of Victoria, Melbourne
Purchased with the assistance of
the National Gallery Society
of Victoria, 1976
Selected by Arts Project Australia

top right:
Harrell Fletcher
Arts Project Australia 2010
colour inkjet print
Collection of the artist,
Portland, Oregon

bottom image:
Harrell Fletcher
Ceramics by Valerio Ciccone and Kelvin Heffernan, Arts Project Australia 2010
colour inkjet print
Collection of the artist,
Portland, Oregon

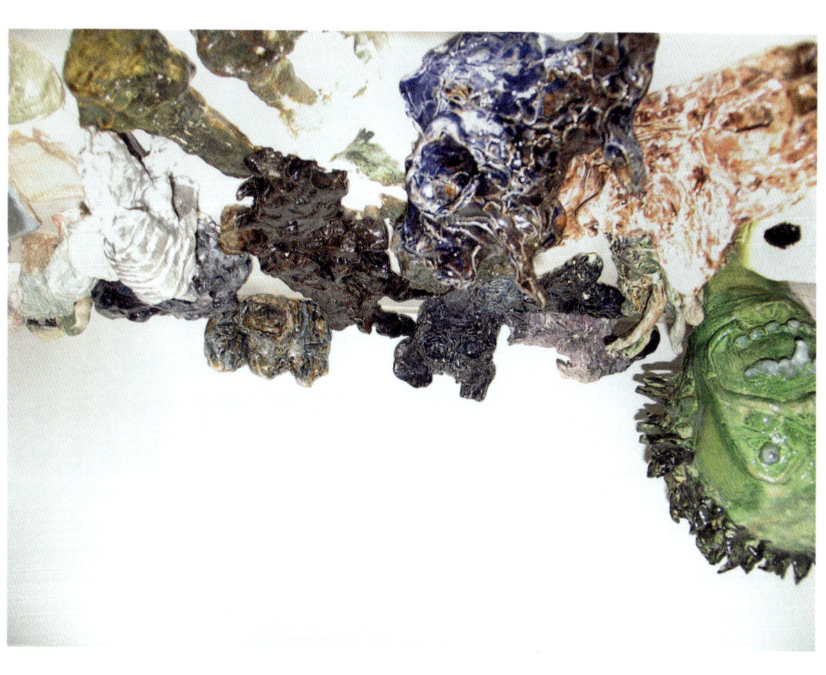

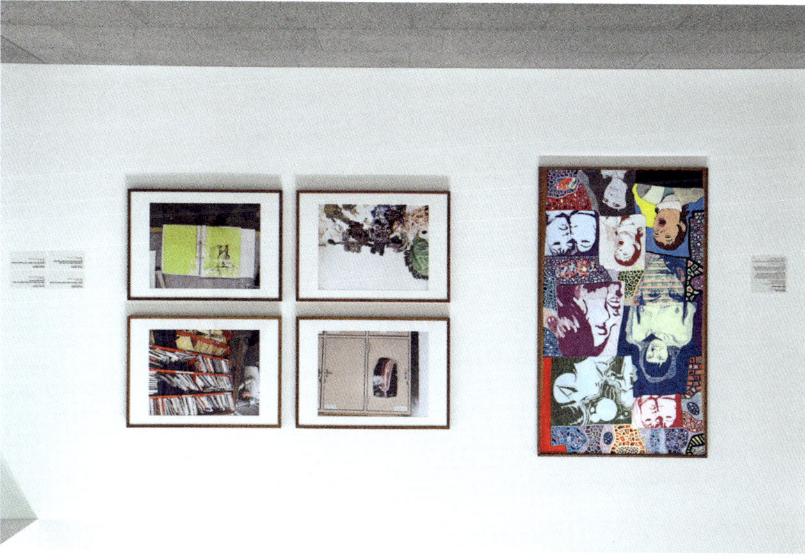

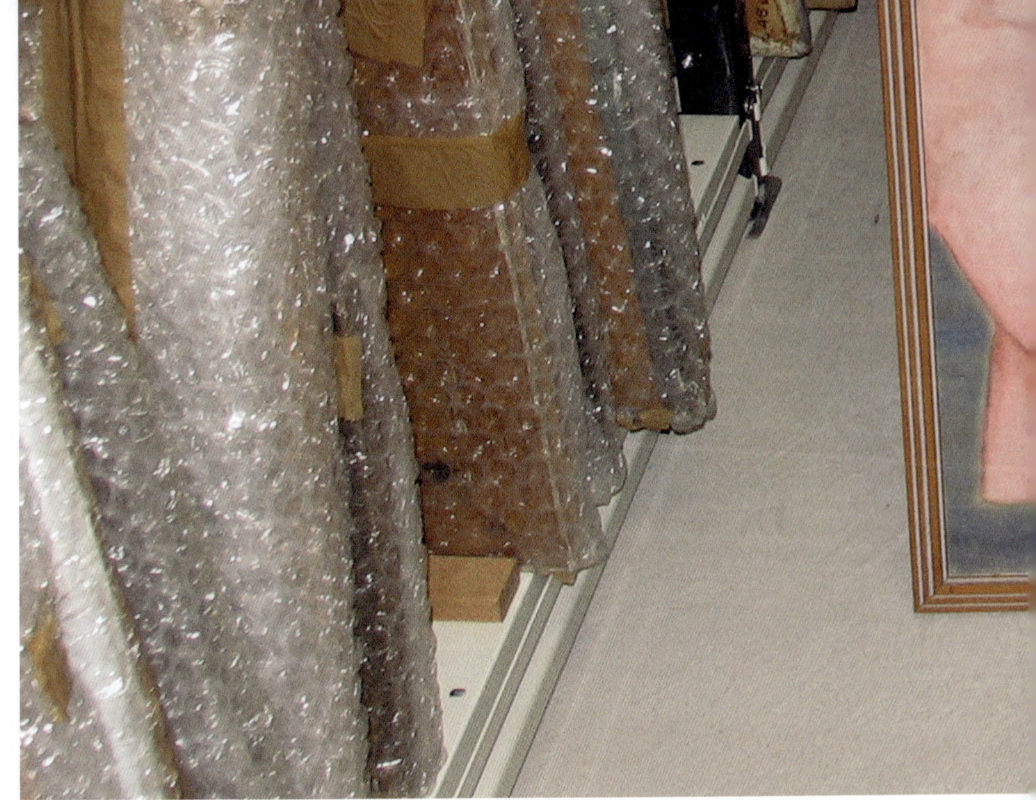

HARRELL FLETCHER

THE SOUND WE MAKE TOGETHER (MELBOURNE)

Percy Aldridge Grainger, 1882–1961, was a prolific composer and a virtuoso pianist with an international reputation. Australian-born, he is remembered as his country's greatest composer. Grainger is well-regarded for his arrangements of English folk song and band music, for music education and for his pioneering efforts in experimental music and instrument innovation. His genius also encompassed an extraordinary facility for languages, a strong talent for design and an innovative approach to museology. The evidence of his creative life forms the Grainger Collection at the University of Melbourne, a portion of which can be seen in the Grainger Museum (re-opening in October 2010), a building that the composer helped design.

GRAING MUSEUM

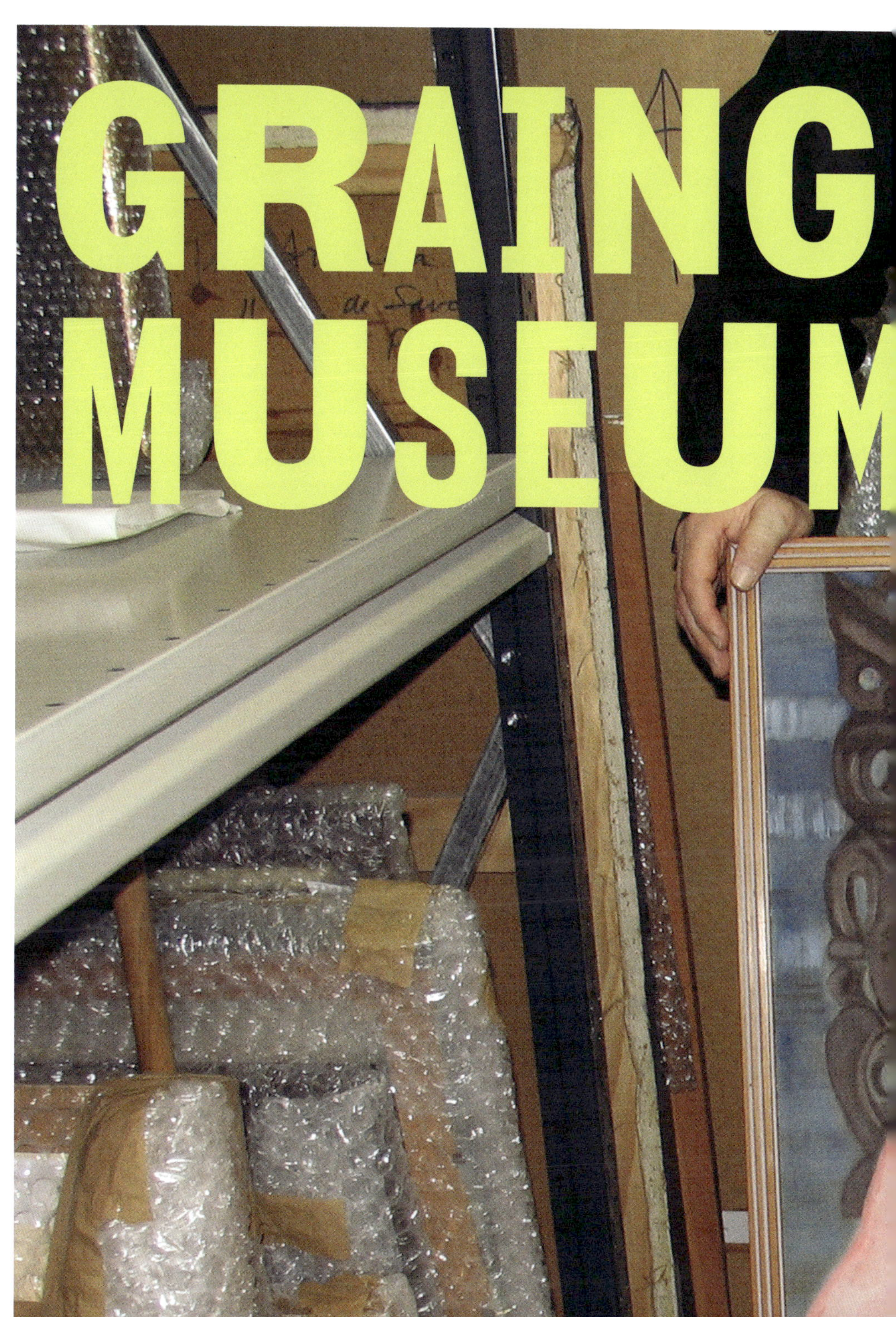

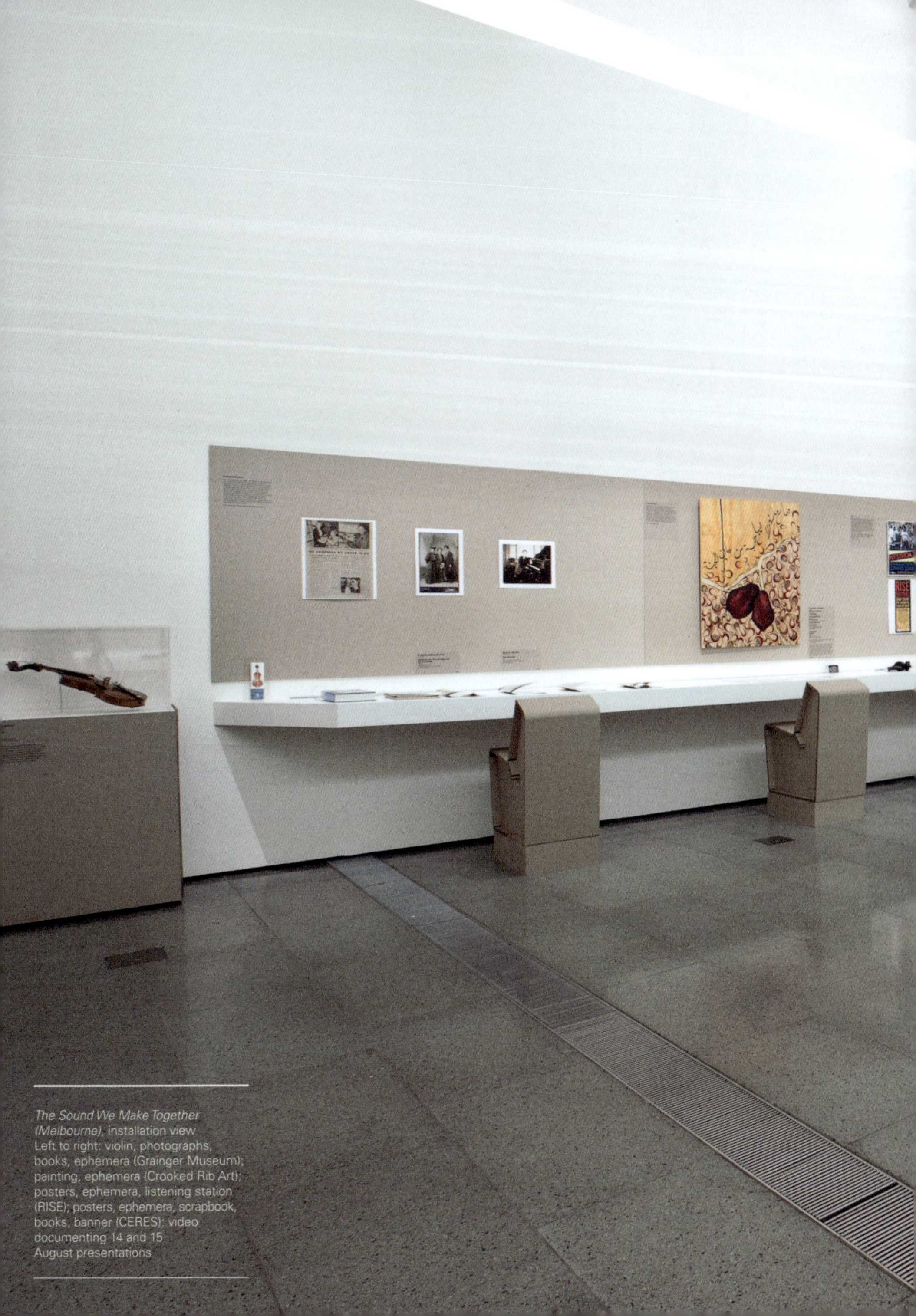

The Sound We Make Together (Melbourne), installation view
Left to right: violin, photographs, books, ephemera (Grainger Museum); painting, ephemera (Crooked Rib Art); posters, ephemera, listening station (RISE); posters, ephemera, scrapbook, books, banner (CERES); video documenting 14 and 15 August presentations

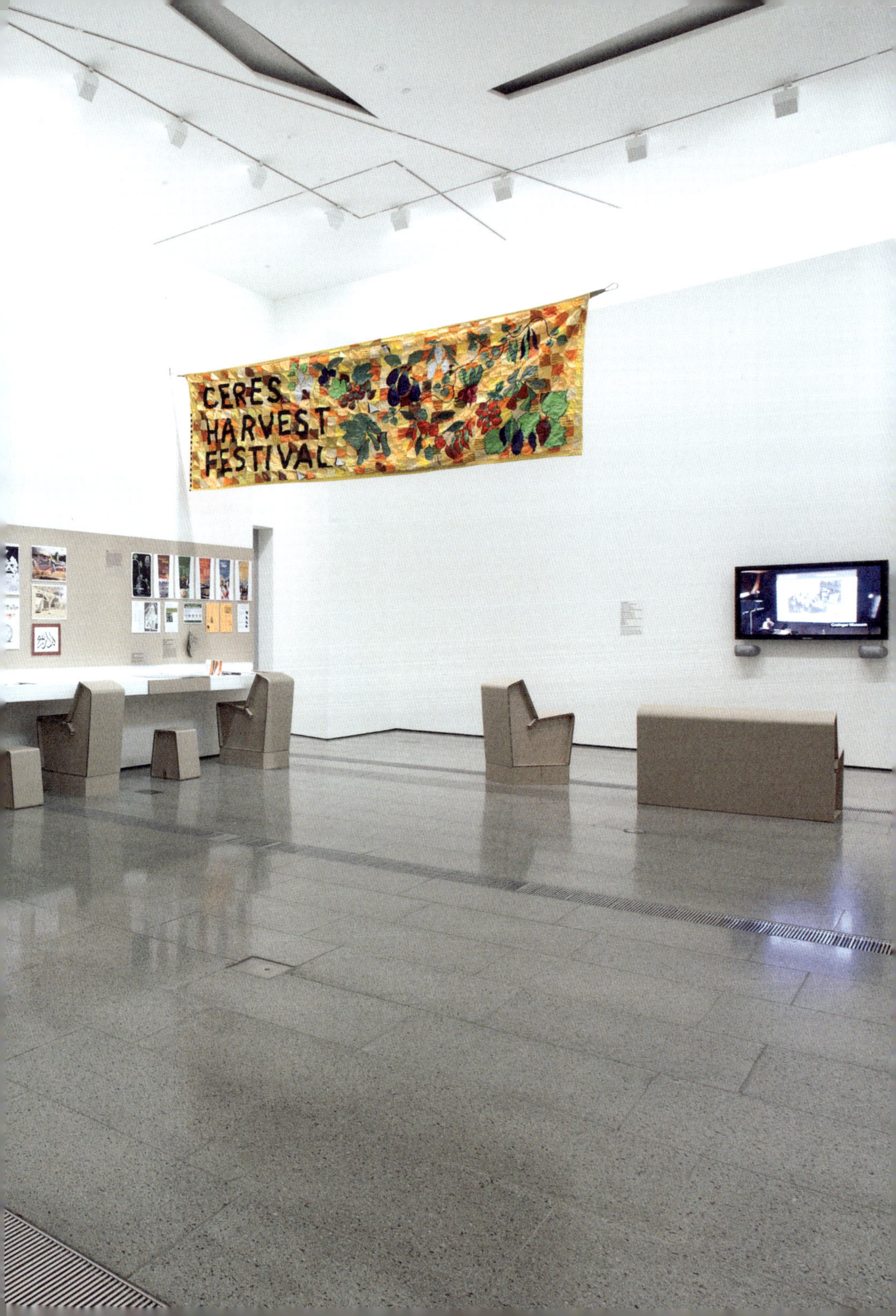
CERES
HARVEST
FESTIVAL

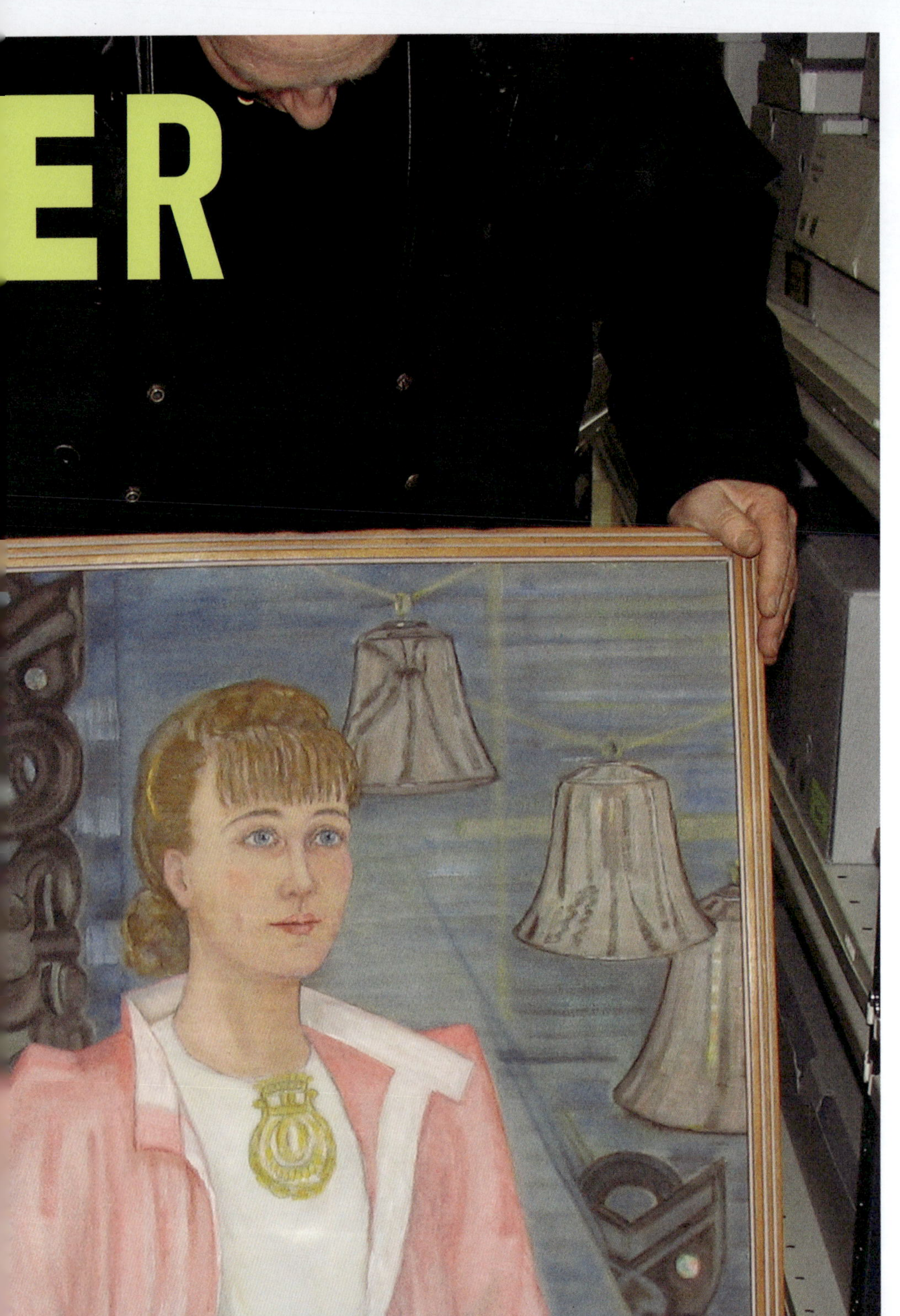
ER

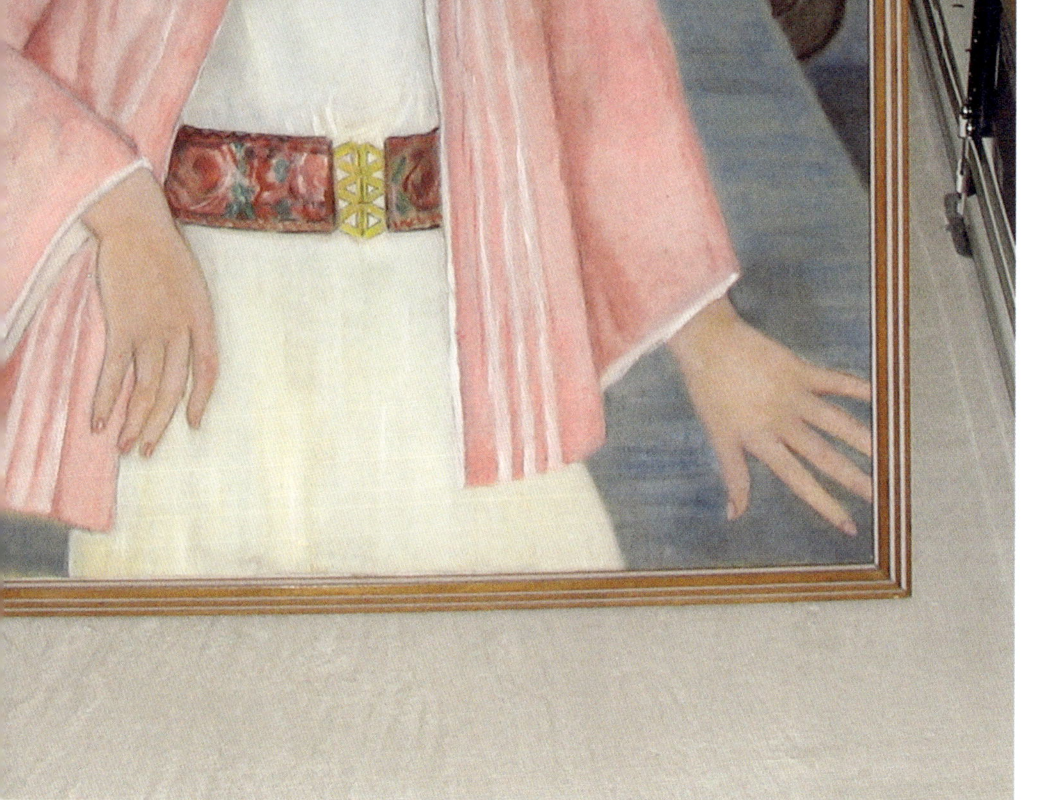

11 SEP – 30 JAN 11

Grainger Museum
The University of Melbourne
Victoria 3010
www.lib.unimelb.edu.au/collections/grainger

Harrell Fletcher
Ella Grainger's self-portrait in towel clothes, Grainger Museum storage 2010 (detail)
colour inkjet print
Collection of the artist, Portland, Oregon

ngv
National Gallery of Victoria

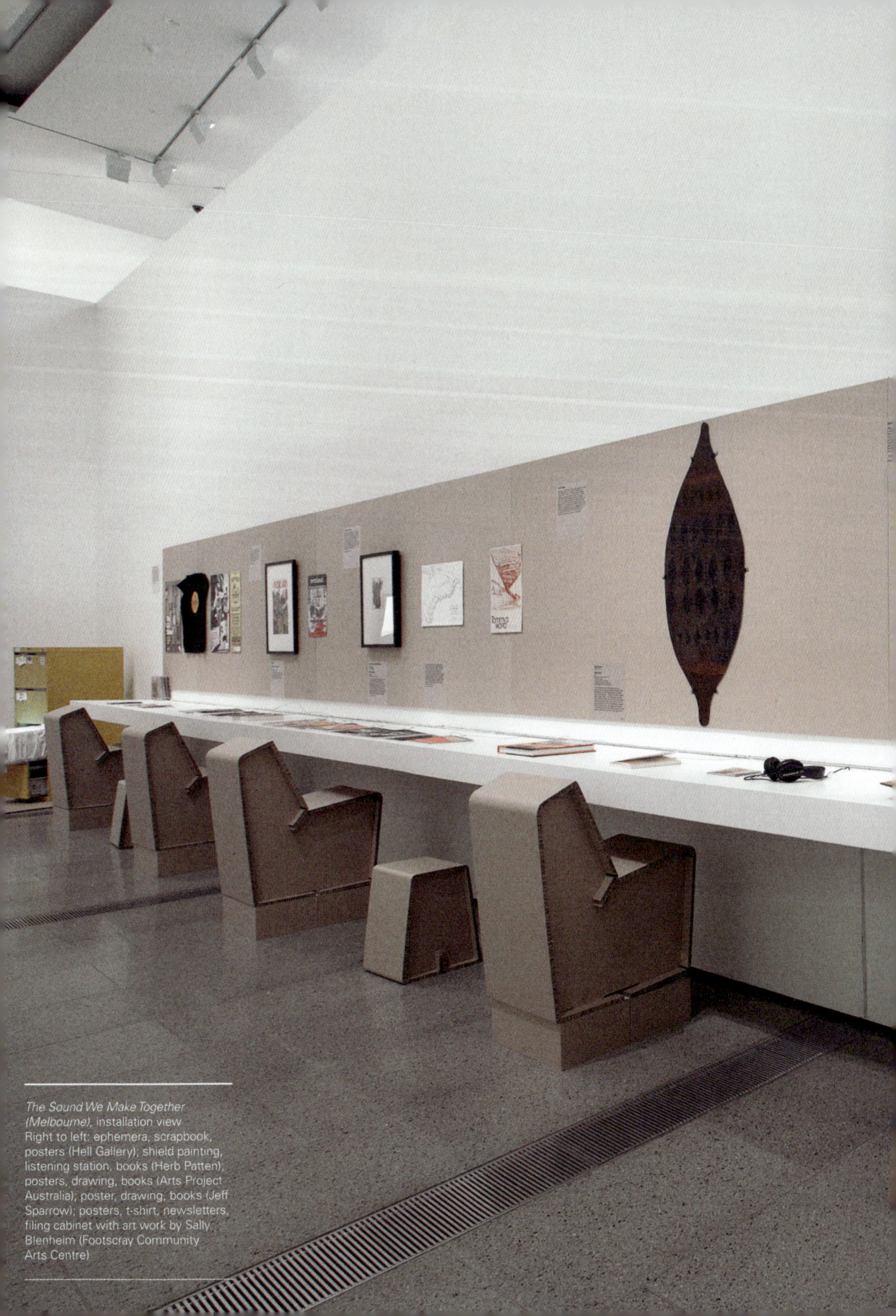

The Sound We Make Together (Melbourne), installation view
Right to left: ephemera, scrapbook, posters (Hell Gallery); shield painting, listening station, books (Herb Patten); posters, drawing, books (Arts Project Australia); poster, drawing, books (Jeff Sparrow); posters, t-shirt, newsletters, filing cabinet with art work by Sally Blenheim (Footscray Community Arts Centre)

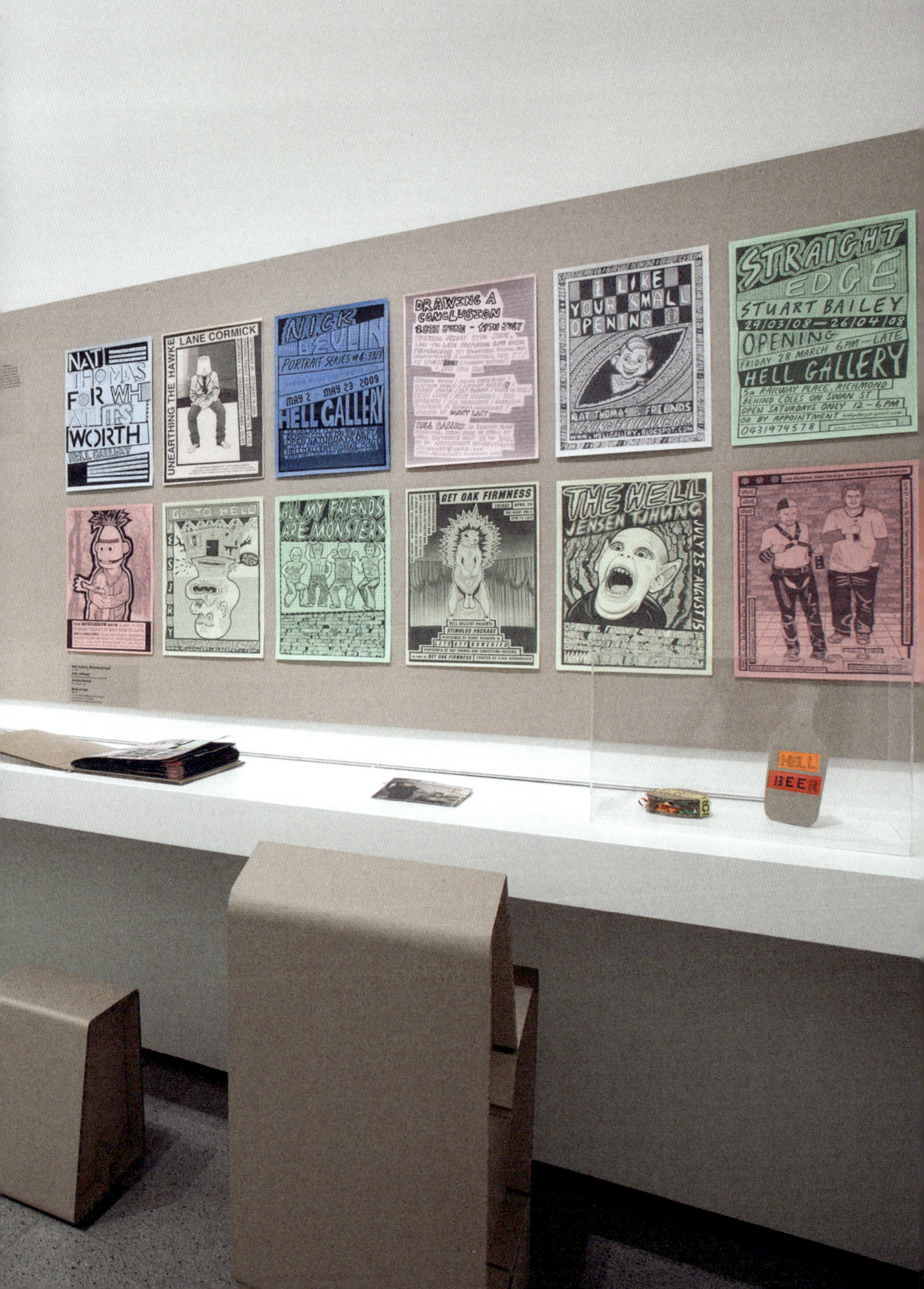
NAT THOMAS
FOR WHAT IT'S WORTH
HELL GALLERY
LANE CORMICK
UNEARTHING THE HAWKE
NICK DEVLIN
PORTRAIT SERIES #4:33/3
MAY 2 - MAY 23 2009
HELL GALLERY
DRAWING A CONCLUSION
28TH JUNE - 19TH JULY
I LIKE YOUR SMALL OPENING
NAT THOMAS & FRIENDS
WWW.HELLGALLERY.BLOGSPOT.COM
STRAIGHT EDGE
STUART BAILEY
29/03/08 — 26/04/08
OPENING
FRIDAY 28 MARCH 6PM — LATE
HELL GALLERY
5a RAILWAY PLACE, RICHMOND
BEHIND COLES ON SWAN ST
OPEN SATURDAYS ONLY 12 — 6PM
OR BY APPOINTMENT
0431974578
GO TO HELL
JESJURY
ALL MY FRIENDS ARE MONSTERS
GET OAK FIRMNESS
FRIDAY APRIL 24
HELL GALLERY PRESENTS
STIMULUS PACKAGE
GET OAK FIRMNESS
THE HELL
JENSEN TJHUNG
JULY 25 - AUGUST 15
HELL
BEER

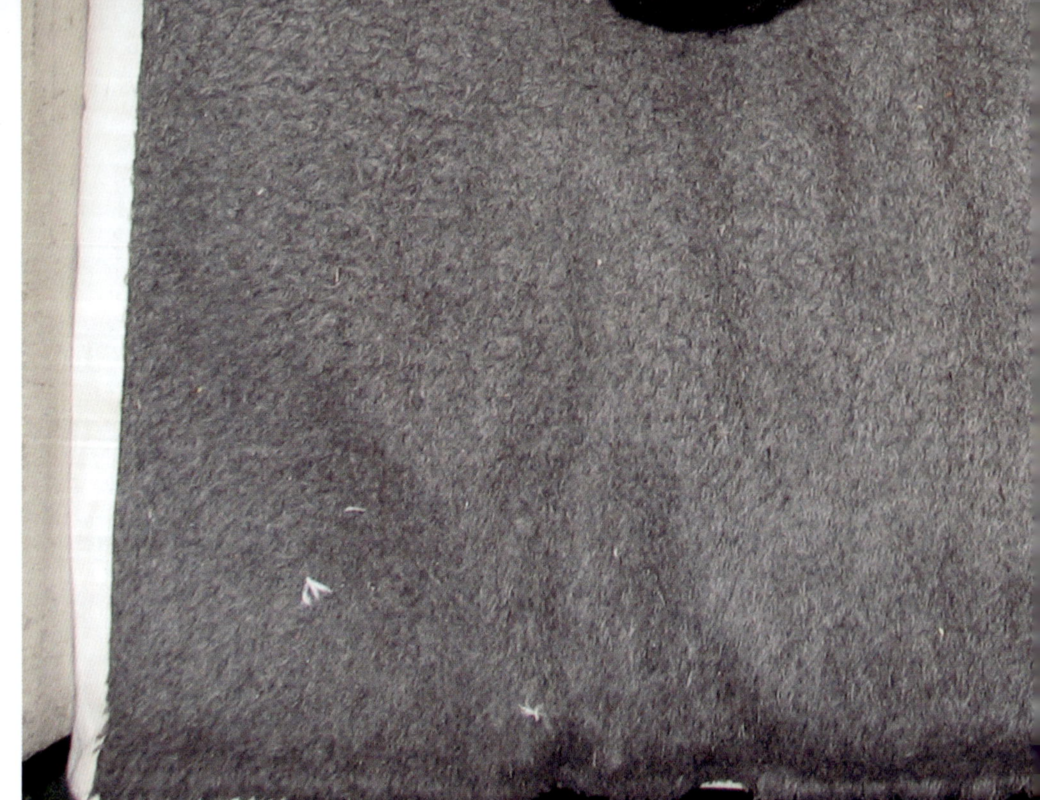

HARRELL FLETCHER

THE SOUND WE MAKE TOGETHER (MELBOURNE)

We built Hell Gallery (founded in January 2008) from materials salvaged from the skips of larger art institutions where we work as freelance art installers. The Hell domain consists of Hell Gallery, Hell Toupee (mini gallery), studios, performance stage, garden bar and barbecue. Hell's stolen motto is 'Build it and they will come' and was born from a desire to eat, play music, dance, watch footy and light fires, all while holding hands with art. Hell is dedicated to our two cats, Mike and Kelly. We love you.

Jess Johnson and Jordan Marani

HELL GA

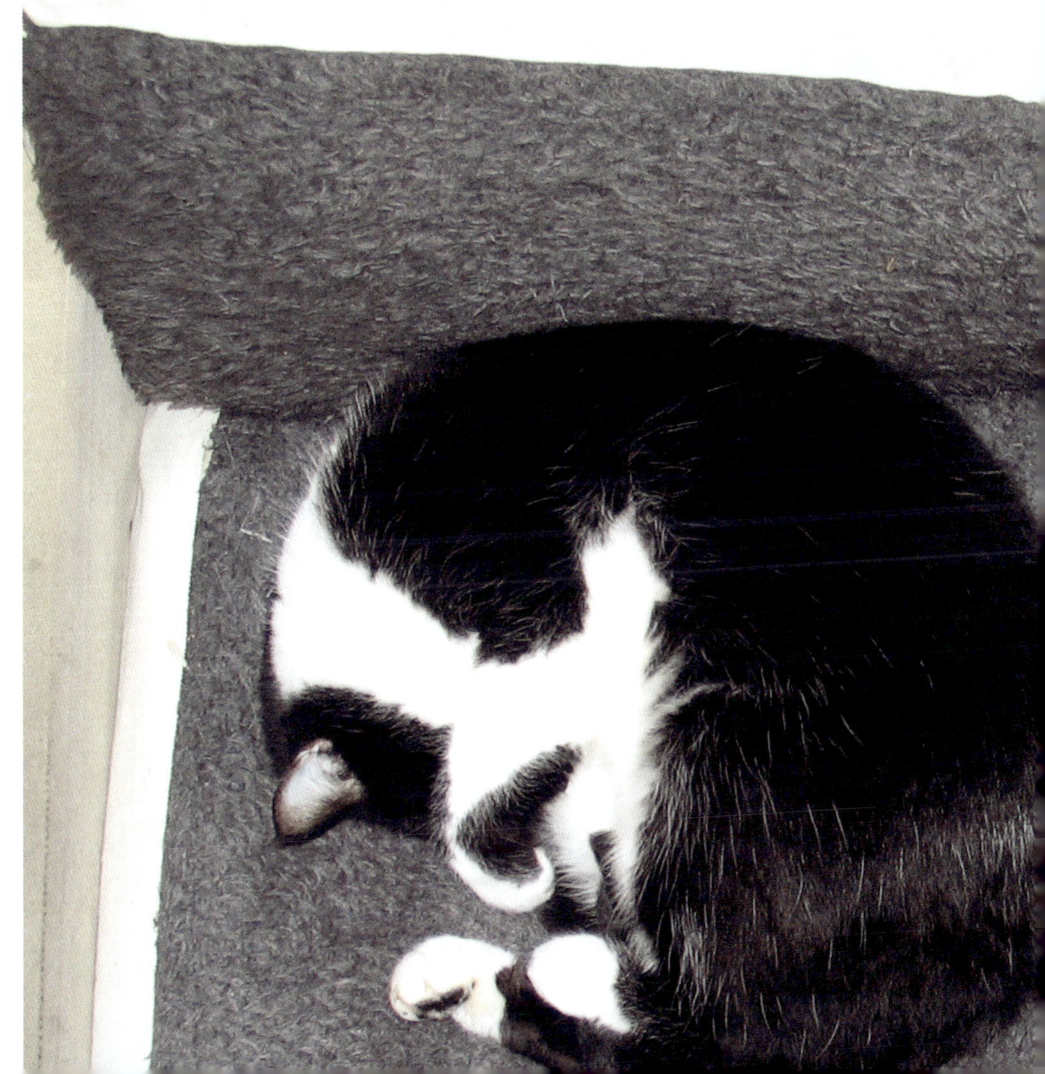

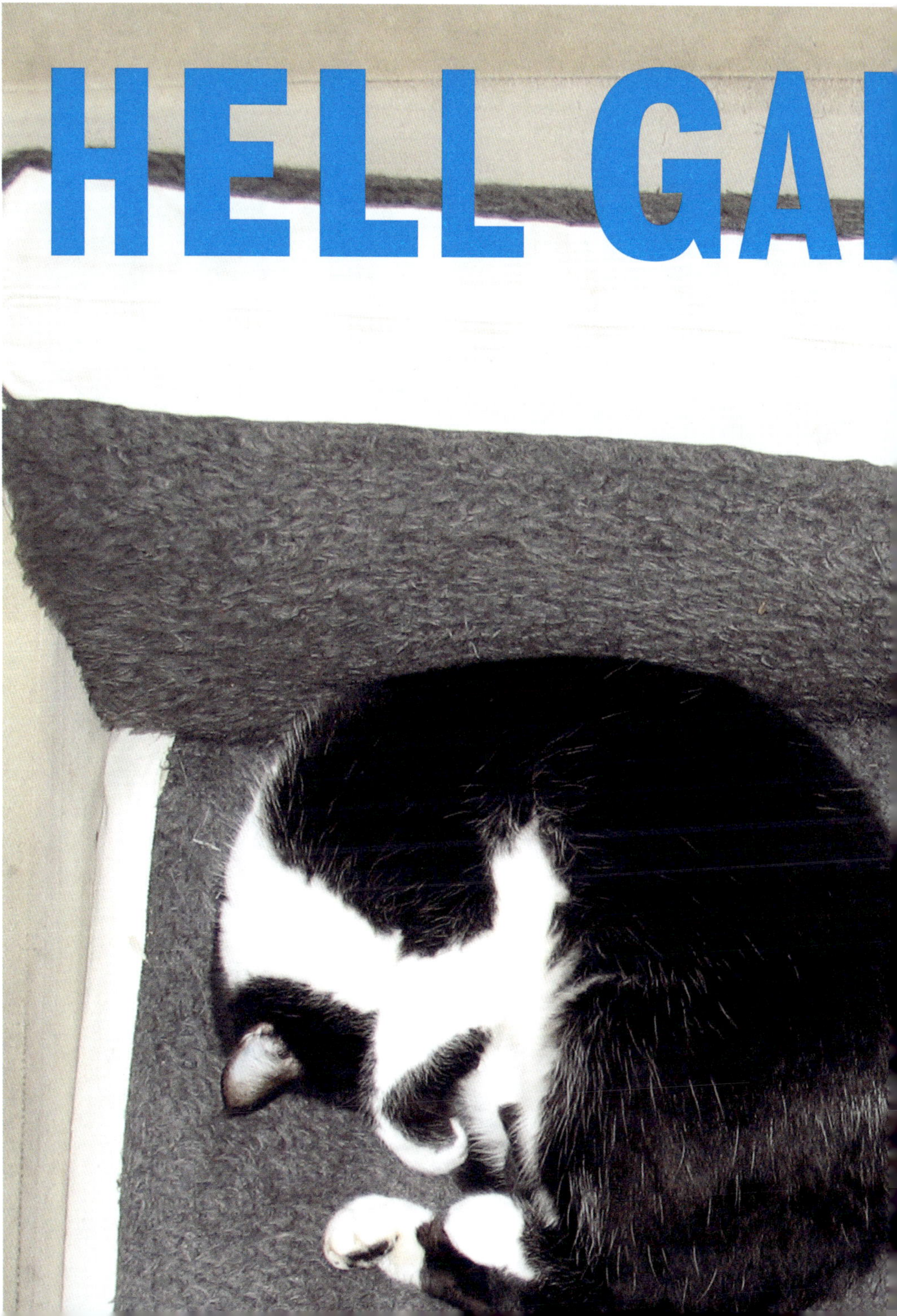

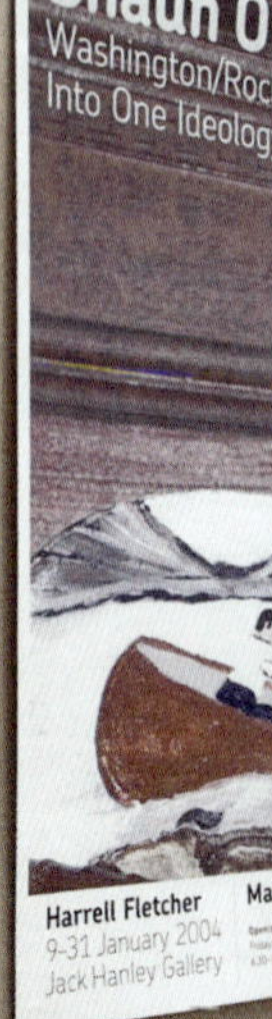
Shaun O'Dell
Memory Extinction
Harrell Fletcher
9–31 January 2004
Jack Hanley Gallery
Maintaining The Jazz
Opening Reception
Friday 9 January 2004
6:30–8:30pm
389–395 Valencia Street
@15th Street
San Francisco CA 94103
www.jackhanley.com
415 522 1623 tel
415 522 1631 fax
Shaun O'
Washington/Rock
Into One Ideology
Harrell Fletcher
9–31 January 2004
Jack Hanley Gallery
Mai

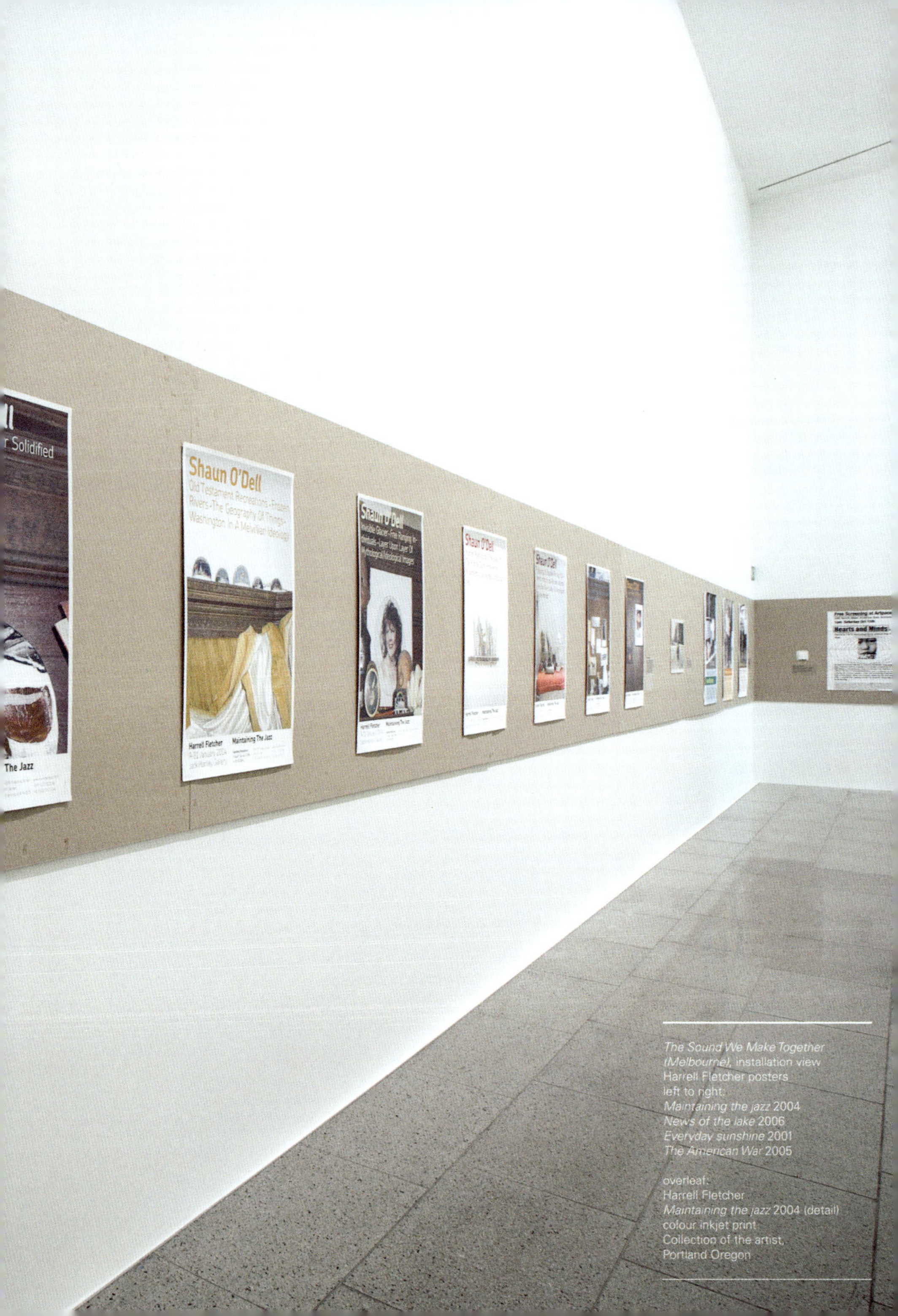

The Sound We Make Together (Melbourne), installation view
Harrell Fletcher posters
left to right:
Maintaining the jazz 2004
News of the lake 2006
Everyday sunshine 2001
The American War 2005

overleaf:
Harrell Fletcher
Maintaining the jazz 2004 (detail)
colour inkjet print
Collection of the artist,
Portland Oregon

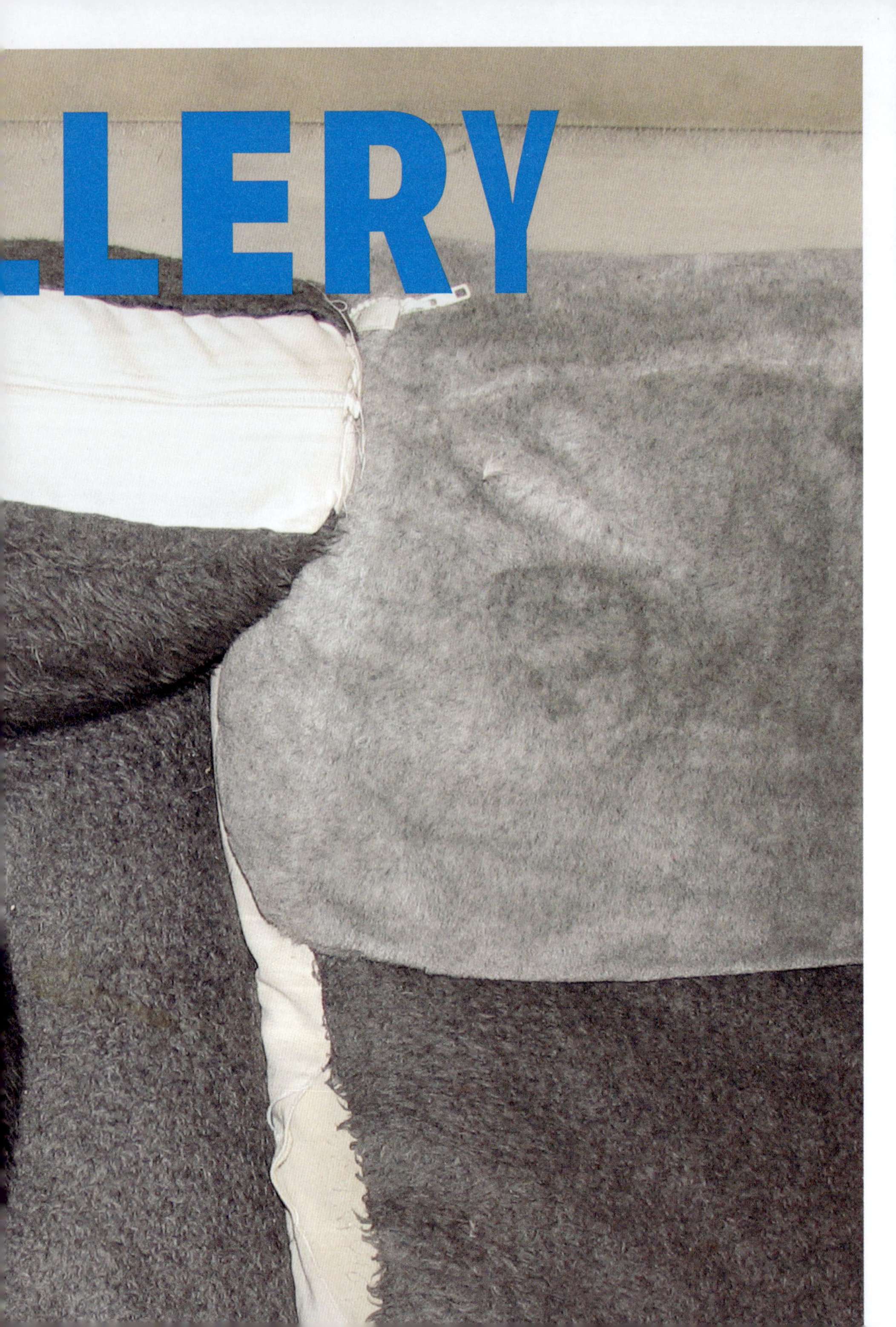
LLERY

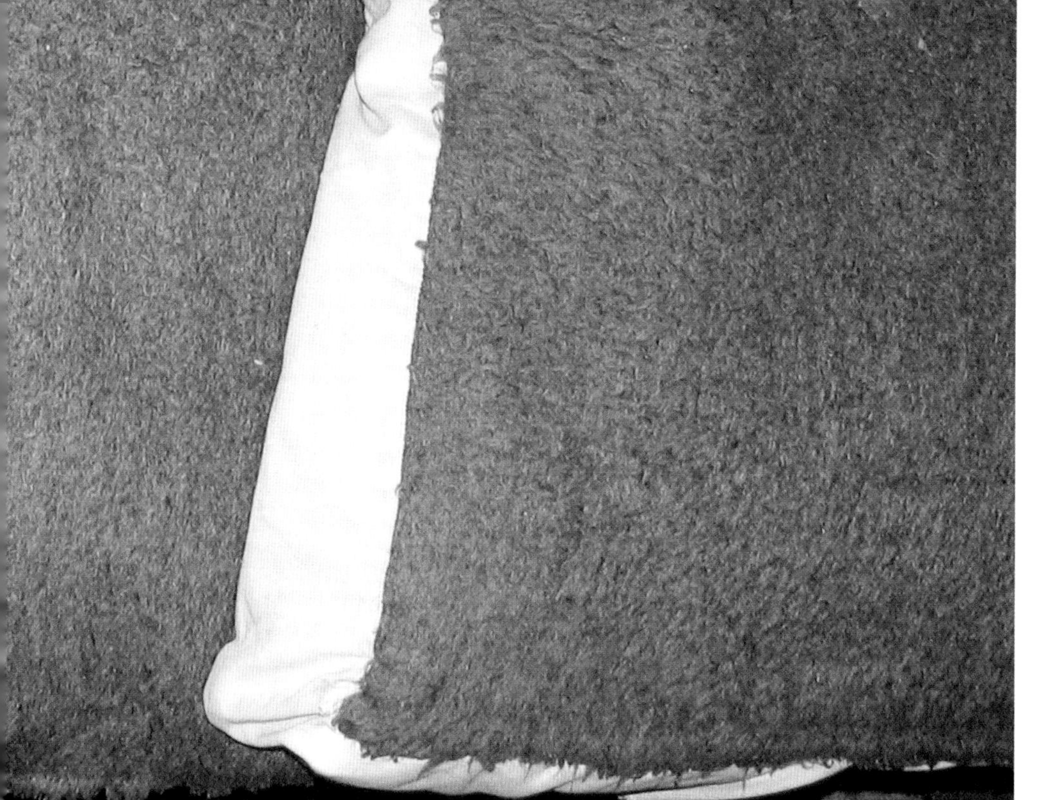

11 SEP -
30 JAN 11

Hell Gallery
5a Railway Place
Richmond Victoria 3121
hellgallery.blogspot.com

Harrell Fletcher
Kelly asleep, Hell Gallery 2010 (detail)
colour inkjet print
Collection of the artist,
Portland, Oregon

ngv
National
Gallery of
Victoria

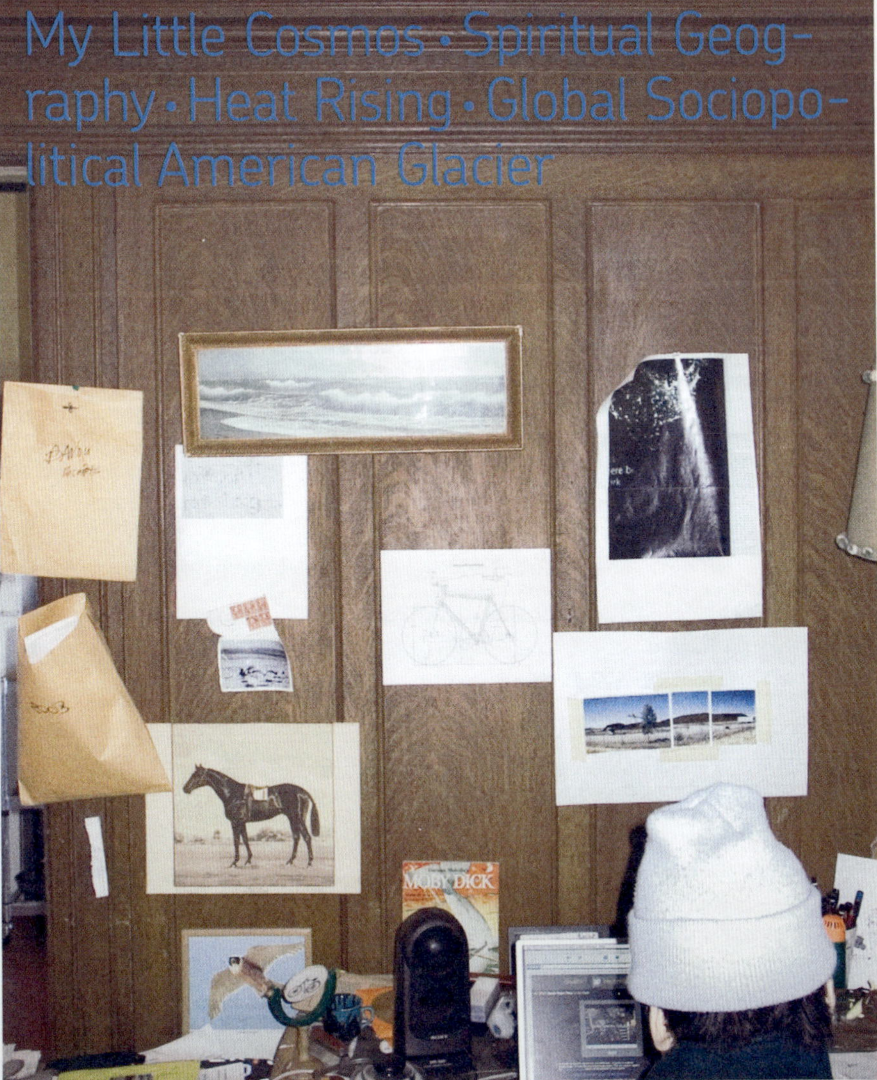

Harrell Fletcher
9–31 January 2004
Jack Hanley Gallery

Maintaining The Jazz

Opening Reception
Friday 9 January 2004
6:30–8:30pm

389+395 Valencia Street
@15th Street
San Francisco CA 94103

www.jackhanley.com
415.522.1623 tel
415.522.1631 fax

Shaun O'Dell

Following In Reverse Through Different Imaginings • Recapitulations • The Ohio River Valley Of American Billionairehood

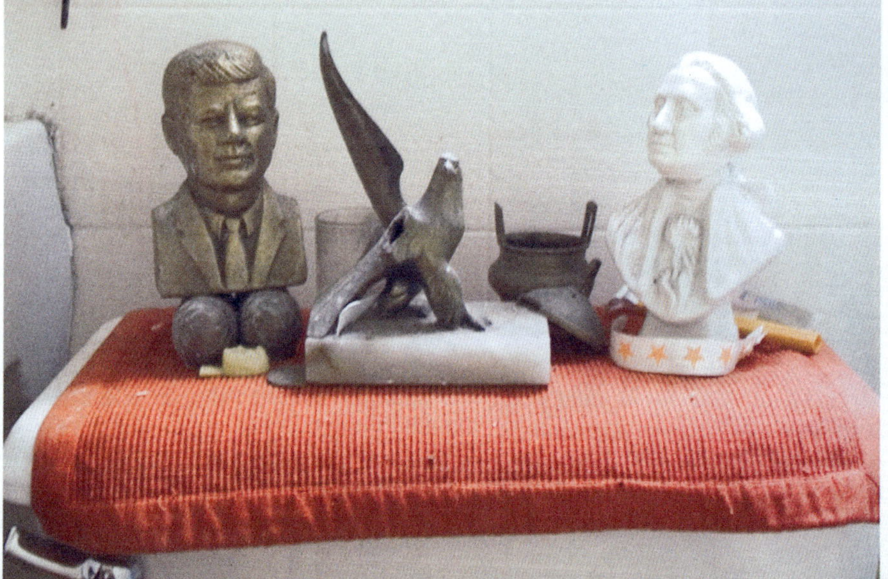

Harrell Fletcher
9–31 January 2004
Jack Hanley Gallery

Maintaining The Jazz

Opening Reception
Friday 9 January 2004
6:30–8:30pm

389+395 Valencia Street
@15th Street
San Francisco CA 94103

www.jackhanley.com
415.522.1623 tel
415.522.1631 fax

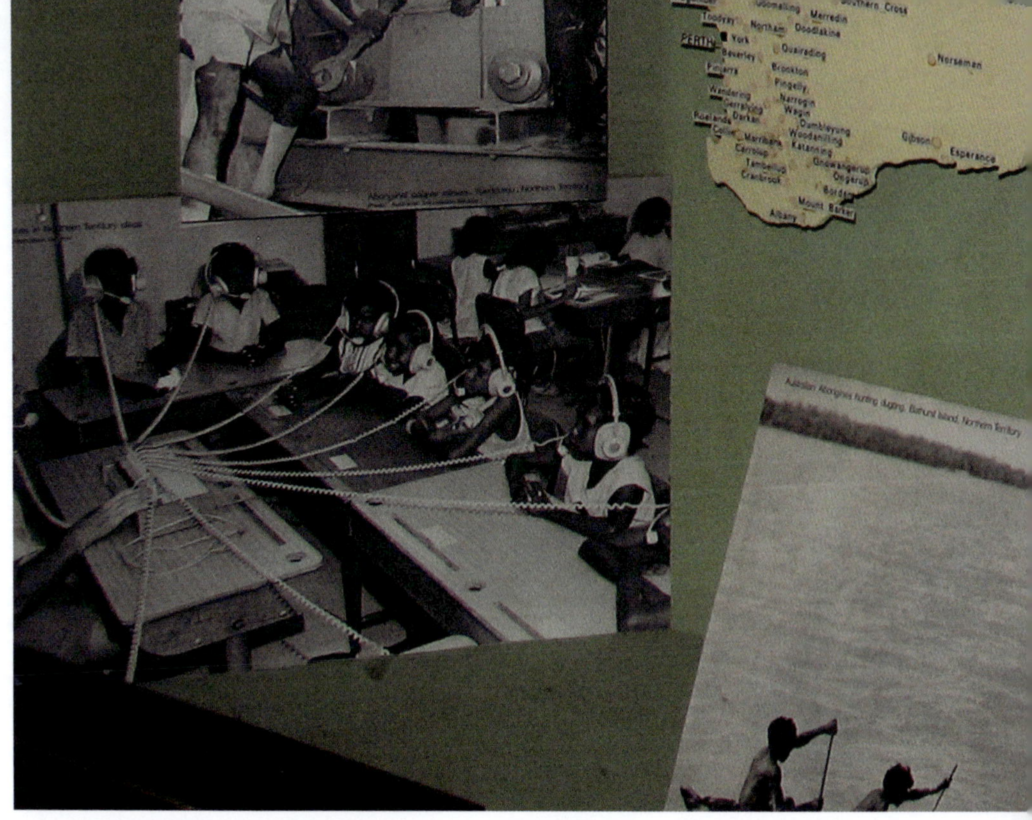

HARRELL FLETCHER

THE SOUND WE MAKE TOGETHER (MELBOURNE)

Herb Patten is a senior Koori elder of the Gunnai/Kurnai people of East Gippsland and the Dhudhuroa/Waywurru people of northern Victoria. He is widely known throughout Australia as a professional gumleaf player (he was a grand finalist on the television program *Australia's Got Talent* in 2007) and has released two CDs, *How to Play the Gumleaf* and *Born an Aussie Son*. Patten received a Diploma in Visual Art from RMIT University in 2005 and completed a Master of Arts degree in 2007 on the Indigenous history of gumleaf playing. A series of five paintings by Patten based on the designs of Indigenous shields from various Victorian groups is in the collection of the National Gallery of Victoria and one is installed in this exhibition.

HERB PA

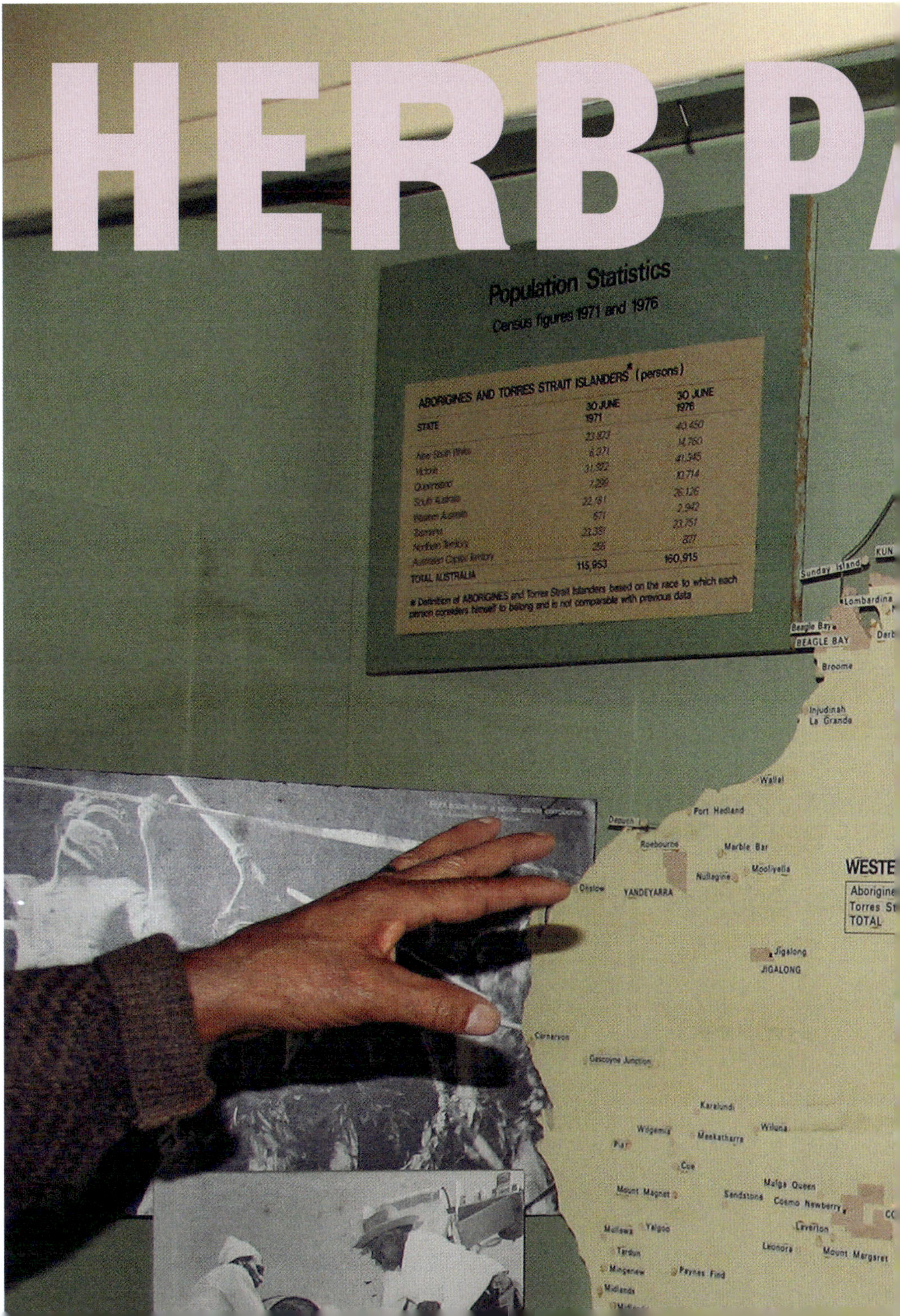

Population Statistics
Census figures 1971 and 1976
ABORIGINES AND TORRES STRAIT ISLANDERS* (persons)
30 JUNE 1971
30 JUNE 1976
STATE
115,953
160,915
TOTAL AUSTRALIA
* Definition of ABORIGINES and Torres Strait Islanders based on the race to which each person considers himself to belong and is not comparable with previous data
Sunday Island
Lombardina
Beagle Bay
BEAGLE BAY
Broome
Injudinah
La Grande
Wallal
Port Hedland
Roebourne
Marble Bar
Nullagine
Mooliyella
Onslow
YANDEYARRA
WESTE
Aborigine
Torres St
TOTAL
Jigalong
JIGALONG
Carnarvon
Gascoyne Junction
Karalundi
Wiluna
Meekatharra
Cue
Mount Magnet
Sandstone
Malga Queen
Cosmo Newberry
Laverton
Leonora
Mount Margaret
Yalgoo
Mullewa
Mingenew
Paynes Find
Midlands

Following a preview of the exhibition on 3 September 2010, some of the participants gathered with Harrell Fletcher and Alex Baker to discuss their thoughts on their involvement. The following is a transcript of that conversation.

Alex Baker, National Gallery of Victoria (NGV): From what you have experienced of the project *The Sound We Make Together (Melbourne)*, what are your overall impressions?

Sue Roff, Arts Project Australia (APA): I had no idea what to expect until we walked in the exhibition space just today. I've probably been less hands-on in terms of my organisation for various reasons, but it's a really great overview of so many different parts of the Melbourne community. Some I was familiar with and some I wasn't.

Harrell Fletcher: Something that I'm really glad about, working with the NGV, is that admission is free so people can come and go as much as they want, which isn't the case in most equivalent galleries elsewhere in which you almost always pay admission, and so people usually only go once. I really like that people can experience this exhibition over a period of time, having a chance to look at different parts on different visits, especially in the case of the video of the weekend of presentations – it's four hours long.

Marg Vandeleur, Centre for Education and Research in Environmental Strategies (CERES): I wouldn't classify this as a community art project – it's some kind of hybrid form of engagement between community and artist. It intersected in some ways very narrowly, and also fairly unrepresentatively, with what CERES is, and I think that's got to do with the length of time of the project ... but on the other hand what it brings together are organisations' perceptions of themselves and how they want to be seen to the world, to some extent; plus, someone who is a complete outsider to us and their take on it, and juxtaposing those two things. So, I suppose it's some kind of hybrid form of community artist engagement, which I haven't encountered before and it will be interesting to see what comes of it.

Harrell Fletcher: Anybody else have thoughts on that?

Reeham Hakem, Crooked Rib Art (CRA): I've been involved in pretty much each component and stage of the project from the start. One component involved us choosing an artwork or an object we thought would represent ourselves or our group. And I just felt, through each component, we were the ones who were curating the exhibit, and I found that really profound because we all have different points of view and different issues that we feel need to be pointed out, whether through art or reading material. That was a really good way of engaging people who are not necessarily in the arts culture, rather than it being the same, static requirements of what an artist is and what it takes to be an artist. And we could all be involved in that sense, having community members curating the exhibit.

Harrell Fletcher: I think that's a really good point and, in the case of Crooked Rib Art, you ended up making a piece of art as well. But if we had required that of everyone, some people would feel really uncomfortable making art, so we didn't want to put them in that position; instead, we found a role that we felt everyone would be comfortable in, which was to choose a piece of art from the NGV's collection. That was a way to allow people to participate in something that they wouldn't normally get to do.

Jennifer Barry, Footscray Community Arts Centre (FCAC): At some point in the process, because each stage of the process did feel like it had its own shape and its own sort of experience, I think it was after you came to visit [laughs] or maybe it was before or maybe we were anticipating the visit – we can't remember – but it was a very anthropological feeling, like a Margaret Mead kind of moment where we were going, 'the man is looking at us through the kind of grilled gates of whatever it is, through the lens of visual art or whatever', and it felt kind of weird and it felt a little voyeuristic and we felt a little like we were kind of quaint objects in and of ourselves, but that was only that one part of the process. The other part of the process like the selection of the NGV artwork and how you want to be represented, and I agree with what Marg said is that it felt more empowering in some aspects or stages of the project and, in other stages of the project, it was like a waiting game of how you felt you were going to be represented. So it was interesting …

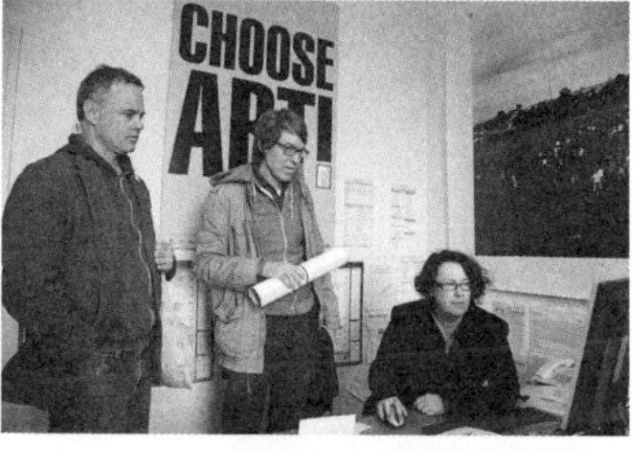

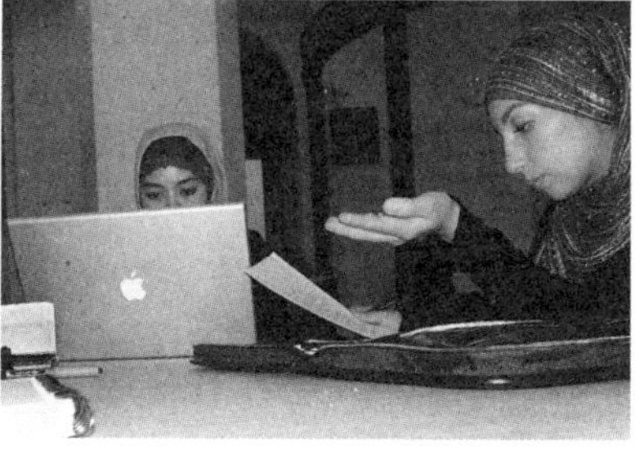

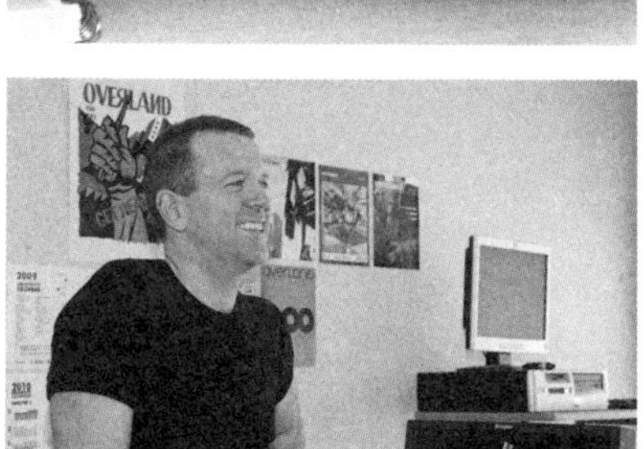

top:
Harrell Fletcher, Alex Baker and Jennifer Barry, Footscray Community Arts Centre

middle:
Reeham Hakem (right), Crooked Rib Art. Photograph by Harrell Fletcher (detail)

bottom:
Jeff Sparrow

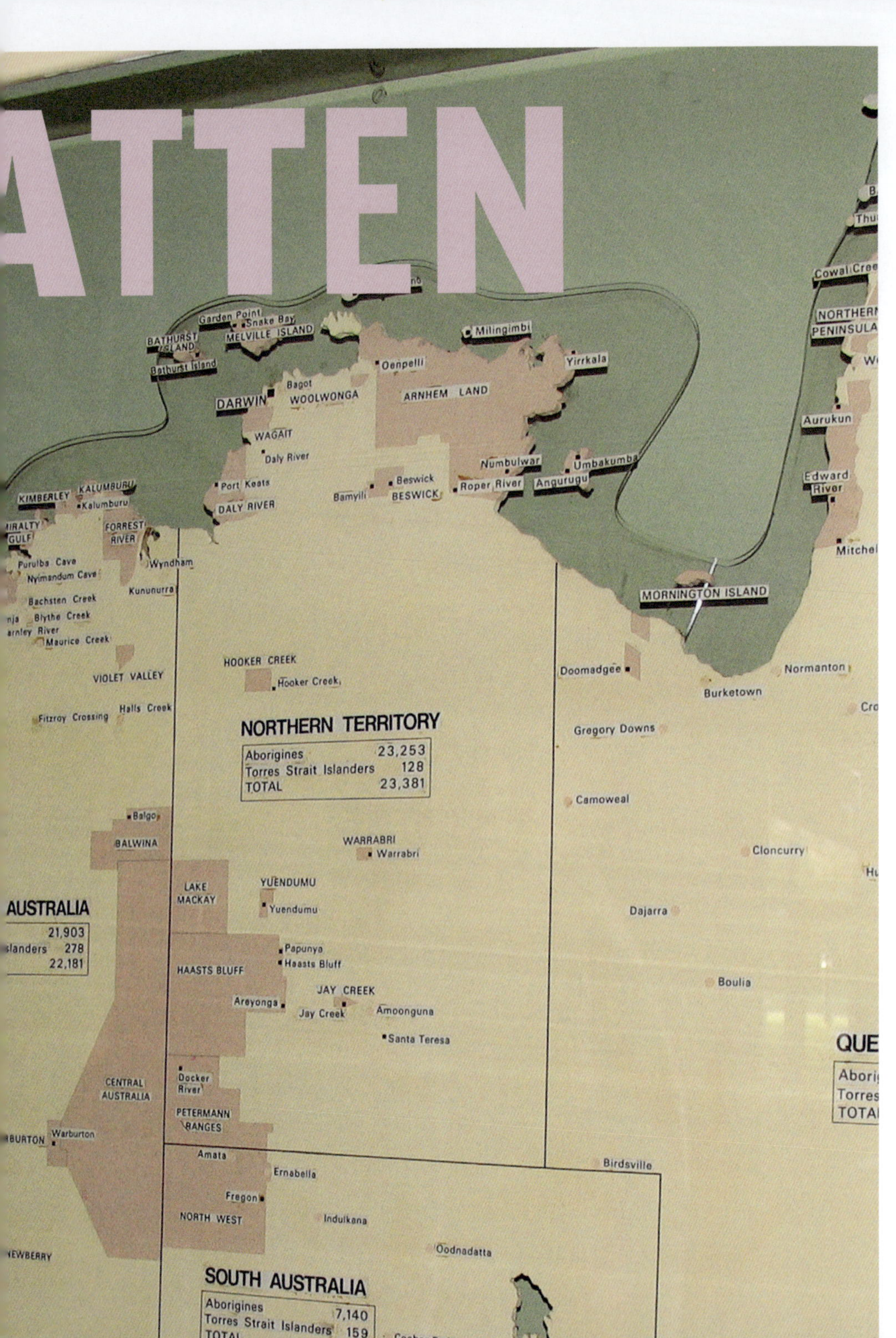
ATTEN
Garden Point
Snake Bay
BATHURST ISLAND
MELVILLE ISLAND
Bathurst Island
Milingimbi
Oenpelli
Yirrkala
DARWIN
Bagot
WOOLWONGA
ARNHEM LAND
WAGAIT
Daly River
Numbulwar
Umbakumba
Angurugu
Port Keats
Beswick
BESWICK
Bamyili
Roper River
DALY RIVER
KIMBERLEY
KALUMBURU
Kalumburu
FORREST RIVER
Purulba Cave
Nyimandum Cave
Wyndham
Kununurra
Bachsten Creek
Blythe Creek
Maurice Creek
VIOLET VALLEY
Halls Creek
Fitzroy Crossing
HOOKER CREEK
Hooker Creek
NORTHERN TERRITORY
Aborigines 23,253
Torres Strait Islanders 128
TOTAL 23,381
MORNINGTON ISLAND
Doomadgee
Normanton
Burketown
Gregory Downs
Camooweal
Cloncurry
Dajarra
Boulia
Birdsville
Cowal Creek
NORTHERN PENINSULA
Aurukun
Edward River
Mitchell
Balgo
BALWINA
WARRABRI
Warrabri
LAKE MACKAY
YUENDUMU
Yuendumu
AUSTRALIA
21,903
278
22,181
Papunya
Haasts Bluff
HAASTS BLUFF
JAY CREEK
Areyonga
Jay Creek
Amoonguna
Santa Teresa
CENTRAL AUSTRALIA
Docker River
PETERMANN RANGES
Warburton
Amata
Ernabella
Fregon
NORTH WEST
Indulkana
Oodnadatta
SOUTH AUSTRALIA
Aborigines 7,140
Torres Strait Islanders 159
TOTAL

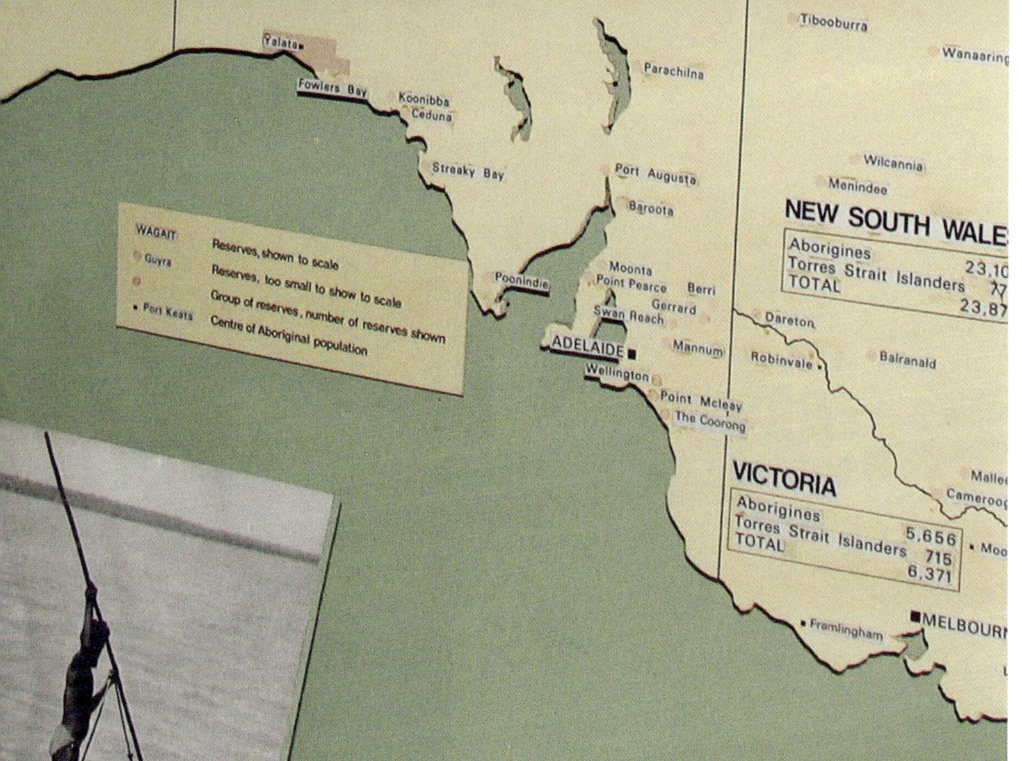

11 SEP –
30 JAN 11

Harrell Fletcher
Herb Patten explaining Aboriginal population map, Aborigines Advancement League, Victoria 2010 (detail)
colour inkjet print
Collection of the artist,
Portland, Oregon

ngv
National
Gallery of
Victoria

Michael Brennan, FCAC: And if I could add to that … an unforseen aspect of the whole project was that it made us look at what we thought the project meant as well, and what we thought that you, Harrell, were after as an outcome. And it made us question what community is and the way you were approaching community, whether it was a concept of community or an engagement of community or a combination of both. We didn't really arrive at an answer, but it was a question.

Jeff Sparrow: When Alex first contacted me my initial reaction was a certain scepticism about my own involvement. I'd never thought of myself as an artist or having any relationship to fine arts, and I must say that, at various points on the way through, I remember asking Alex, 'How is this going to work? What am I doing? [laughter] What role am I playing?' But by about the second stage, I gave up worrying and just enjoyed the process, and I thought poking around in the back of the NGV was kind of awesome. It was a really good experience in and of itself. Likewise with the weekend on which we all presented talks … Everyone spoke really well and said interesting things and they were groups that I would normally not have had any contact with. It was good for me to have that experience of letting go of any control and saying: these people know what they're doing … something will come of this.

Harrell Fletcher: I really appreciate that people were willing to participate because a lot of trust had to go into believing we were going to, in the end, represent people in ways they would feel comfortable with and that it would be a positive experience for them. A few people have commented that there were all of these different aspects, and so some of them put people in the role of curator; some of them in the role of subject and being of observed and, I actually talk about this in the wall texts on the photographs I took when I was in Melbourne, that we were also asking you all to come to the institution and get a look into the back room so you could have another view of the NGV, different than what you would normally have, and then that was reversed when I got to go and look in your back rooms. So you all were able to have different angles and experiences within the project. Hopefully the audience for the exhibition will also be able to perceive these different perspectives to try and understand you as individuals and groups based on what is on view in the exhibition.

Sim Luttin, APA: I was in communication with Alex from the beginning of the project as well, but what I found was such a wonderful process for it, and I echo what everyone else has said as well, is that you felt part of something big and you felt part of a community even when you didn't know necessarily the other parts of who that community was. I knew some of the organisations and individuals, and others I didn't, but it was very nice to go on a journey where you didn't have a predefined outcome of what that was, so what it allowed the project to do was evolve in these other ways that involved a lot of people from our organisation and a lot of people from other organisations who may not normally get involved in a process such as this, and again who may not be artists. For Arts Project artists to be involved in a project where they got to make a selection from the NGV's collection, got to go back behind the scenes of the NGV and then welcome Alex and Harrell back into the behind-the-scenes at Arts Project, I think was a really unique way of involvement.

Paul Hodges, APA: I just had fun being able to go into the storage rooms and it was a real experience from 10 o'clock to 2.30 or 3.00 o'clock looking through many famous paintings and actually being able to choose a painting from the huge collection. It was a real privilege, and I think the piece we chose was actually quite funky and different from the other ones we saw – more like Pop Art – and it seemed like an appropriate selection.

Marg Vandeleur, CERES: What I was trying to say before is that I don't think we really had either the resources or the time to really engage with and involve our many communities in the decisions we made. But that would have been a completely different project if we were to really get that kind of connection with all the communities CERES represents.

Michael Brennan, FCAC: That's an indication of the fact that it's just impossible to be truly representative of anything or anyone as a group. I think we at Footscray Community Arts Centre are quite aware of that as well because we deal with a number of diverse and different communities and you can't be everything to everyone. I just think that this project shows how much of an important role subjectivity plays in everyday interaction.

Marg Vandeleur, CERES: It's interesting, because I think the choices from CERES's point of view were absolutely apt and I've got no quibble. It's fantastic and the other thing that's interesting is the way the images that were chosen by the organisations and the images that Harrell came up with or selected somewhat echo each other, even though there was no known relationship before you entered into that process. This would be a different sort of project entirely, but I would have loved to have displayed the painting we've chosen at CERES. I know there would have been security issues, but we could have built a project with schoolkids taking photos...

Monica Syrette, Grainger Museum (GM): We've had quite a different experience because we're not a community arts organisation, we're a museum that's within a university and it's primarily an autobiographical museum of quite an unusual person. So it's interesting to hear your perspective about how to engage with your, for want of a better word, stakeholders – the people who use CERES and that you wish to communicate with. When Alex first contacted us I was really

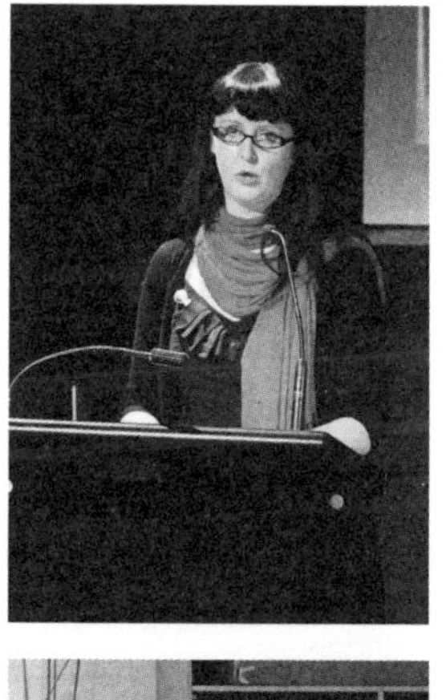

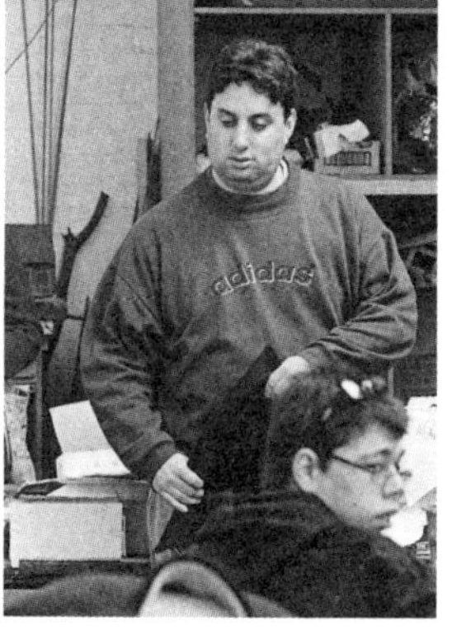

top:
Sim Luttin, Arts Project Australia

bottom:
Paul Hodges, Arts Project Australia

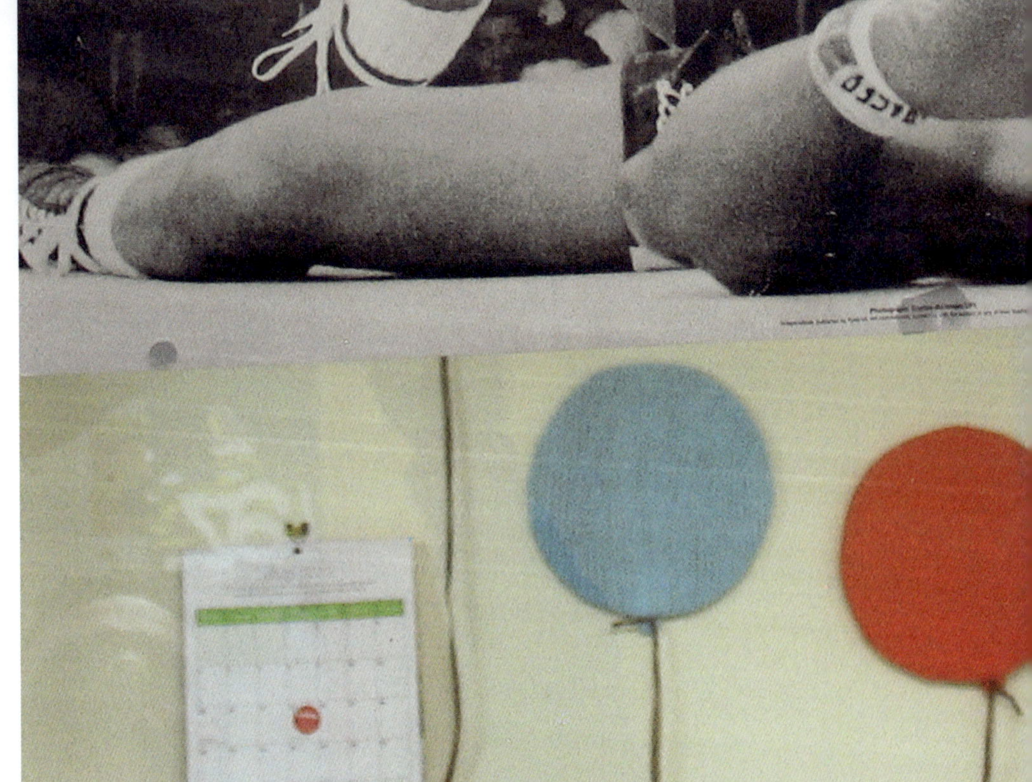

HARRELL FLETCHER

THE SOUND WE MAKE TOGETHER (MELBOURNE)

RISE (Refugees, Survivors and Ex-Detainees) is a not-for-profit incorporated association that enables refugees to build new lives by providing advice, engaging in community development, enhancing opportunity and campaigning for refugee rights. RISE advocates on its members' behalf to improve government refugee policies and to generate positive social change in respect to attitudes impacting on refugees. RISE's settlement service, coupled with music and arts projects, seeks to address the various barriers to successful settlement and empower refugee communities to be active participants in the wider society.

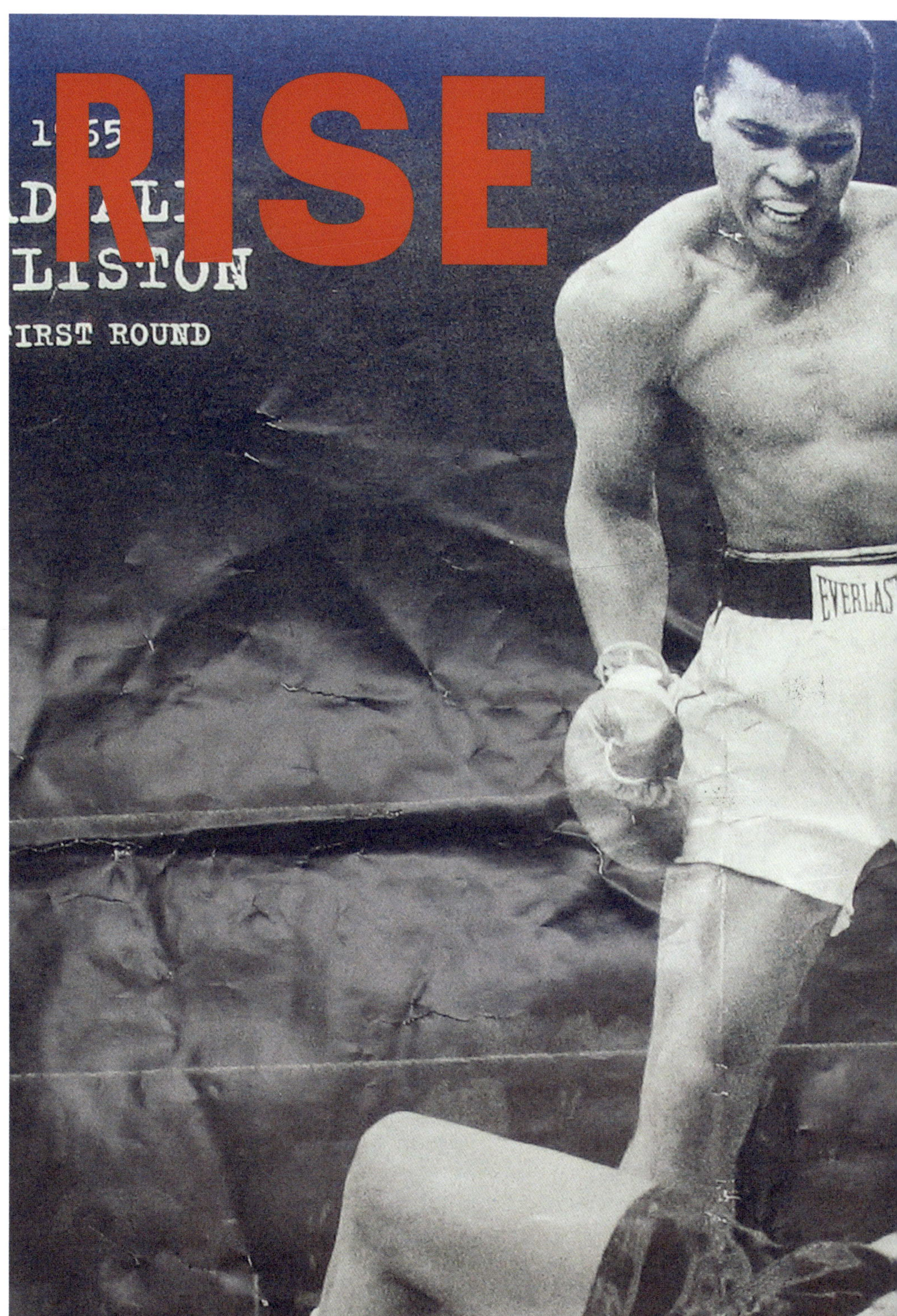
RISE
LISTON
IRST ROUND
EVERLAS

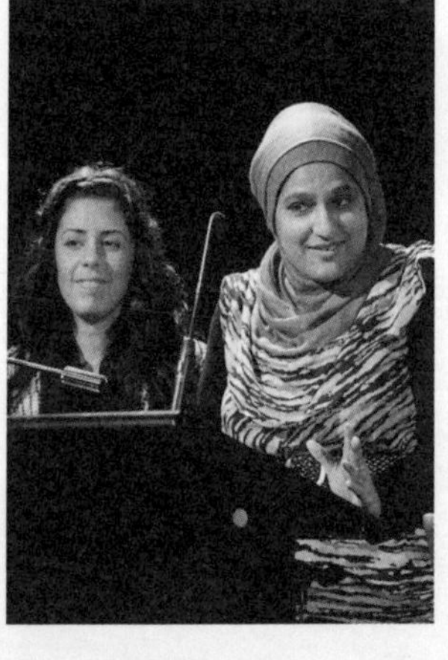

top:
Monica Syrette, Grainger Museum

bottom:
Sumaya Asvat (right), Crooked Rib Art

excited because I knew Harrell's work and I felt there were real parallels with Grainger and what Harrell is interested in. Grainger wanted to make music democratic and explore music as a universal language. I find it interesting to hear how everyone here had different perspectives and expectations about the project. I was also at NGV storage on the day that Jeff Sparrow was there making his selection, and after we had been looking around he said to me, 'I don't know why I'm here, I don't know what's going on'. He was really confused [laughter], I sort of just jumped in.

Jennifer Barry, FCAC: We did enjoy the high art/low art divide, not that there is one, but we enjoyed playing with the NGV because we don't usually get to do that, so you know, that's kind of fun …

Marg Vandeleur, CERES: It was a thrill for our people too. It was the highlight.

Alex Baker, NGV: Both Marg and Jennifer raised really interesting questions, which was something I was going to ask you about. What is the role of a large public institution like the NGV – an encyclopedic art museum – in fostering an exhibition like this? What happens when a project such as this occurs in a large institution such as the NGV? What's been really interesting for me as a curator is working within my institutional structures to realise a project like this. It's been a challenge, but it's also been rewarding because we have tremendous resources here that other institutions do not necessarily have. For instance, a vast collection that we could use in interesting ways as a conceptual backbone for the Fletcher project involving you all. In another case, the photographs that Harrell took here in Melbourne were printed and framed onsite at the NGV. Could that happen at a smaller art institution? And maybe the show would have taken a different direction if it was indeed at a different kind of institution, at a community arts organisation like Footscray. Does anybody have anything to say about this?

Jennifer Barry, FCAC: I reckon definitely the different resources available. As soon as I walked in the space this afternoon, the level of resources that the NGV can bring to even the display of an exhibition itself is profound compared to what we can do at Footscray. In terms of the content, in terms of the concept and the process, it would very much, I think, fit in with what Footscray Community Arts Centre does; it's all about people and communities and self-identity or how you would like to be represented and the discussions around representation, so we would love to do this kind of project, so if the NGV maybe just gave us the money and then we could do the next one.

Sumaya Asvat, CRA: I think that's the point; it's really powerful to have an exhibition like this in an institution like this, not just for the artists but for the viewers. I'll take my artist's hat off and put my educator's hat on, so when kids or youth come here, they can see art in a different way. It becomes really real; it's tangible. It's not something – 'Oh high art is this and these sort of artists do this', but it's something that everyone can be a part of, and so they come in and they say, 'Oh I never thought of them as artists but hey, they're working with this group', and for them I think it's also, and for me as well, it's really refreshing to come to an institution like this and see an exhibition that's not egocentric, that's not about one person or one group; it's about everyone working together, so I think that's a power in this whole thing.

Marg Vandeleur, CERES: This is going to sound weird Harrell, but your aesthetic actually makes more sense in this context too, right. If I look at the three pictures you chose to represent CERES, I first thought to myself, 'Oh my god, they're so ugly, you know, why is he selecting to take a photo of a little sign of a little worm when there's so many beautiful things on site?', but in the context of high art, your images and your aesthetic and the juxtaposing of them makes sense. They confront our notions of what's beautiful and what's ugly. I mean, that's what you've done with our images. You've given us three images that on first glance you think, 'My god they're so – well, I thought – they're so ugly!'

Harrell Fletcher: But actually in CERES's case they were all things that you use to represent yourselves with, because these are displays that you use.

Marg Vandeleur, CERES: Of course, but we've got millions of idiosyncratic little things representing us. The whole site is a kind of kaleidoscope of that ...

Jennifer Barry, FCAC: There's a kind of approval stamp that comes with an exhibition like this being at the NGV, but I hate that as well. I hate the fact that it's got to be in a 'cultural institution' in order to be seen as art in some way.

Michael Brennan, FCAC: To try and extend what you're saying, if the exhibition that we've just seen upstairs was presented in one of our own organisations, it could run the risk of being swallowed up by the other activity that happens around it. And while the clean white box of the art institution is often criticised as a very controlled, very institutionalised exhibition space, to my mind it does have the benefit of eliminating distractions so that the subtleties can come to the surface and so you do see those more nuanced ways that the organisations work and the details of the individual organisations have a chance to surface in that kind of isolated space.

Sim Luttin, APA: I was going to say something similar. We're obviously an arts organisation so that sort of clean, crisp space of white walls is more familiar perhaps to us than it is to CERES and other organisations, but walking into the space there was a sense of familiarity somehow about it, that again it did allow the space for these little moments to come to the surface. The moments that Harrell actually captured of us are really familiar things in our environment, and while they're perhaps not the most obvious that we might use to promote ourselves, it really does reveal something about the inner

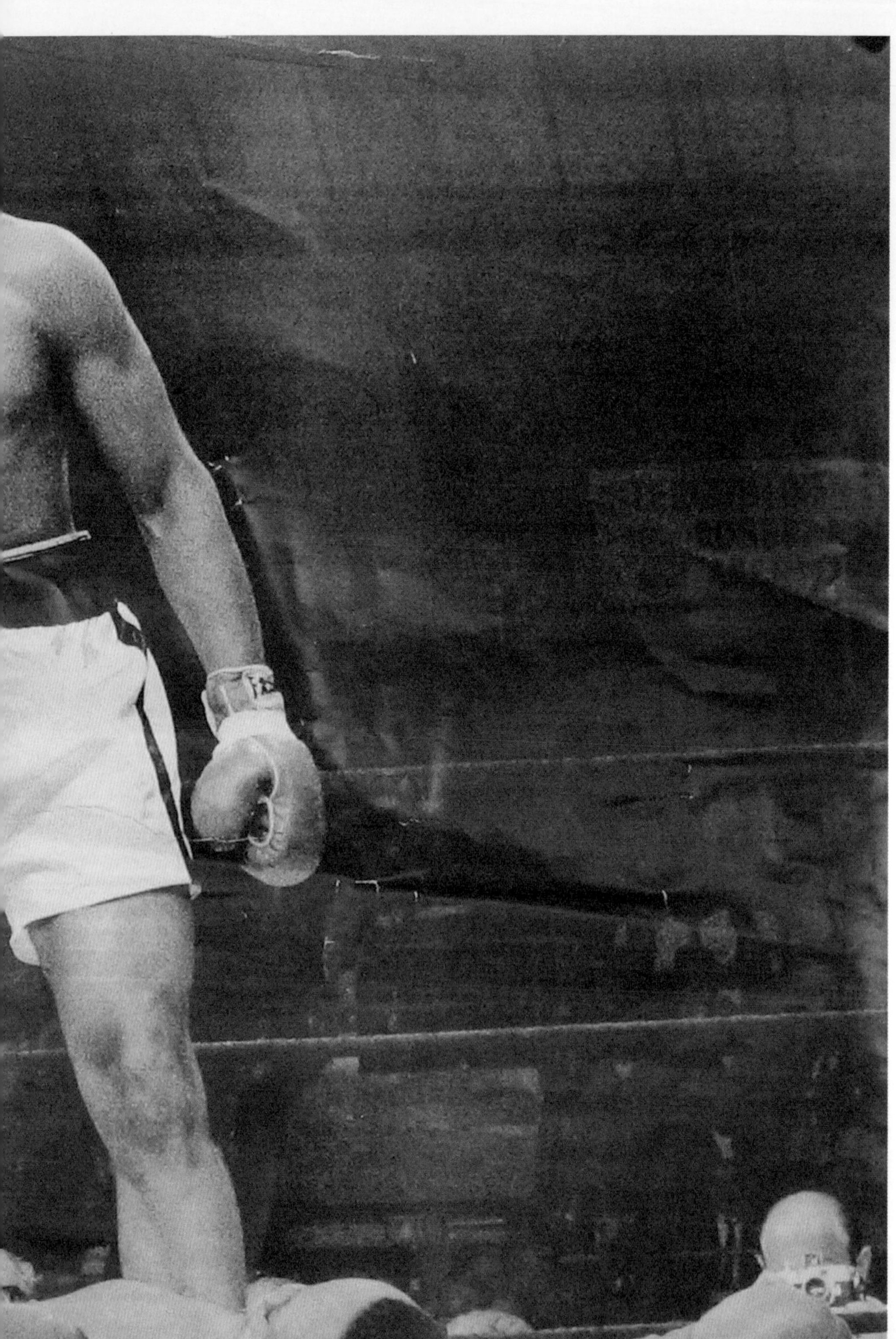

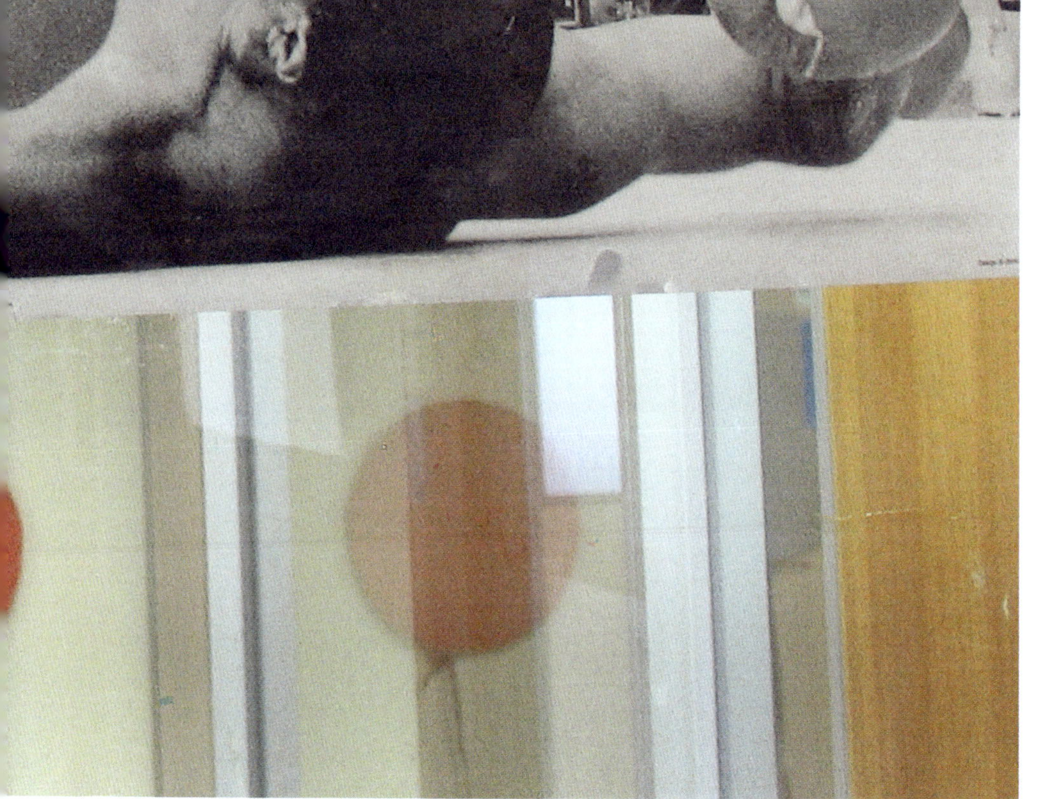

11 SEP -
30 JAN 11

RISE
247 Flinders Lane
Melbourne Victoria 3000
www.riserefugee.org

Harrell Fletcher
Muhammad Ali poster,
RISE office 2010 (detail)
colour inkjet print
Collection of the artist,
Portland, Oregon

ngv
National
Gallery of
Victoria

workings of the organisation and the artists and what we're about. Seeing the small pieces that Harrell picked up on; those idiosyncrasies are quite beautiful moments, I think, in our studio.

<u>Jennifer Barry, FCAC:</u> Alex, did the NGV learn anything from us?

<u>Alex Baker, NGV:</u> We did. During the weekend of presentations there were NGV colleagues in the audience up and down the hierarchy and across different departments and they commented to me about how meaningful an event this was. I'm an outsider to Melbourne and I learned so much about what's happening in this city as a result of this project. Given that I am a contemporary art curator, I often do only contemporary art–related things: art openings, gallery visits, studio visits. I don't necessarily get to go to places like CERES as part of my job, so in many ways by working with Harrell I got to see and experience things that I hadn't seen and experienced before. And by extension, we are exposing both the NGV and its audience to a range of activities that would normally not be engaged with by this institution.

<u>Monica Syrette, GM:</u> I do think it's great to have the project at the NGV because it is very challenging for people to see exhibitions like this that involve the high art versus low art debate. I think that in Australia as well, when it comes to art, people are still very threatened by this debate. This will generate a lot of conversation and that's really great, but it's fantastic that the NGV trusted you as a curator and Harrell as the artist to do this type of project.

<u>Marg Vandeleur, CERES:</u> They also trusted those community organisations that participated to deliver on their end and I think if there's any feedback for the NGV, it's just how valuable and exciting it was for us community organisations to connect with the NGV in that way.

<u>Reeham Hakem, CRA:</u> It works both ways. The NGV gave us a role in creating this exhibit, with our take on what we think should be shown and exhibited, so I think the NGV was great for that initiative. But I also think it worked the other way because now, people coming to the NGV have another reference for when someone mentions 'community art'. Community art is sometimes seen as an excuse for amateur art, for example, and the NGV is a good venue to explore these assumptions. So it worked both ways and I'm really interested to see what's going to happen later on and what sort of questions and discussions are going to come up.

<u>Jennifer Barry, FCAC:</u> Alex, are you going to capture what the audience, how the visitors might respond to the exhibition?

<u>Alex Baker, NGV:</u> It's a good question. I have not really thought that through and it is an ongoing problem in all art museums – gauging visitor responses in constructive ways, providing feedback loops, so to speak.

<u>Harrell Fletcher:</u> I think there will be plenty of opportunity for lots of different things to happen. And something that's happened just during the time that I've been here

is that we've been able to arrange for a few extra things like bringing in The Hacketts to perform as part of the opening tonight, which is just something that came about because we actually went over to Footscray Community Arts Centre and met and heard the band rehearsing in a studio. If you are compelled or interested, either try to work with the NGV or put on your own event and have a conversation in which people talk about this project and their various thoughts and feelings on it. I think one thing that's good to keep in mind, it's been brought up a little bit, is that this exhibition is just one project, it can't do everything. Sometimes I think when an unorthodox project happens, suddenly everyone wants it to be everything to everyone. Most other exhibitions are following the orthodoxy. They're just straight studio art and nobody has any expectation of these exhibitions doing anything other than being what they are. But if projects of this nature were more common, if projects like what we have done here were even just 10% of what museums were showing, then you could start to get a diversity of different levels of engagement and topics. I hope that when people encounter projects such as this one they will have their views expanded about what an artist can do, what a curator can do, the possibility of site-specific engaged projects, etcetera.

Jennifer Barry, FCAC: I think what you do has an anthropological kind of element to it.

Harrell Fletcher: But it also turns a lot of those conventions on their head. An anthropologist usually takes their findings back with them to their university and may not share it with the people they studied. By presenting my projects in the places and with the people who actually live there – they get to participate and engage in various ways that wouldn't normally happen in anthropology – in those ways for me I am addressing the potentially negative, problematic aspects of anthropology or ethnography. I think there's a lot of value in anthropology, but there are ways it could be modified that would make it less problematic and I guess that's what I'm attempting to do. But I have no background as an ethnographer or anthropologist. I'm just an artist.

Michael Brennan, FCAC: Because if you were an anthropologist I suppose you'd try and draw conclusions from your findings, so is that something which is part of your process?

Harrell Fletcher: No it's definitely not, other than in a very subjective way. For me, what makes me who I am, is that I'm someone who is growing and learning and having hopefully a greater understanding and empathy through these project encounters. I'm having real-world experiences rather than just going off my idea of Australia or my idea of young Muslim women or whatever it happens to be; instead, I now have real experiences that change the way I think, drastically. When I'm able to sit back and realise whatever my assumptions were and then compare them to what I've learned, and how I understand these things now, I feel really fortunate in having been able to have first-hand experiences in so many different places and with so many different people.

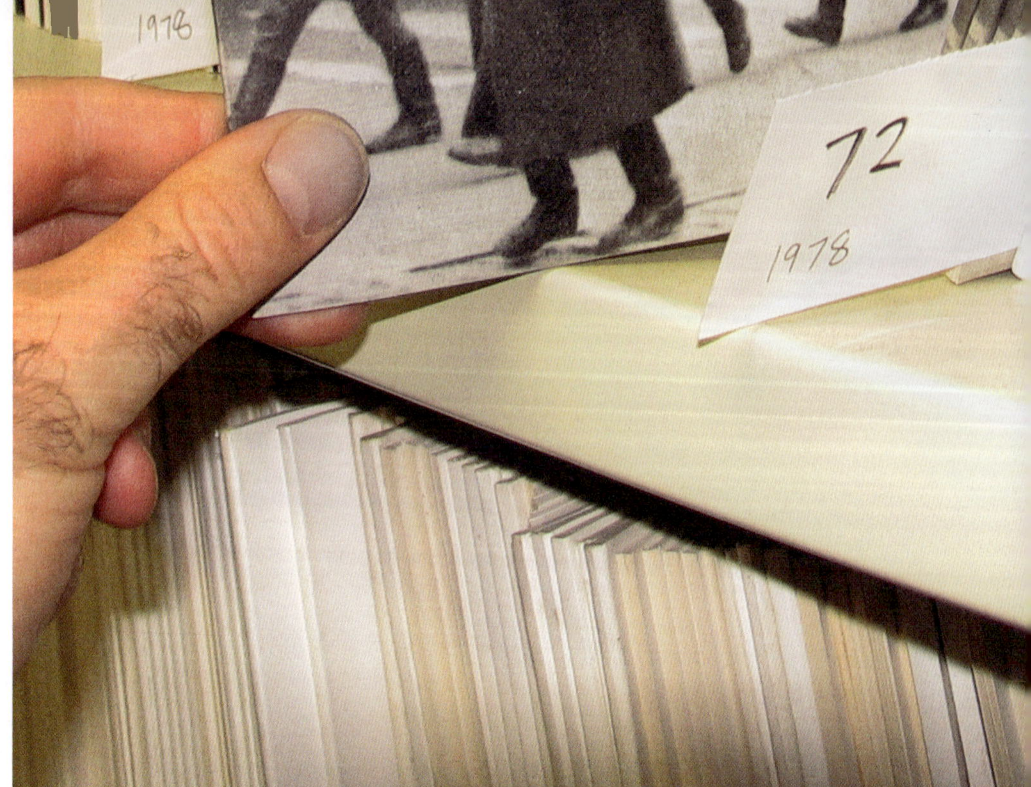

HARRELL FLETCHER

THE SOUND WE MAKE TOGETHER (MELBOURNE)

Jeff Sparrow is the editor of *Overland* literary journal and a research fellow at Victoria University. He is the co-author of *Radical Melbourne: A Secret History* and *Radical Melbourne 2: The Enemy Within*, and author of *Communism: A Love Story* (shortlisted for the Colin Roderick Award) and *Killing: Misadventures in Violence* (a finalist in the Melbourne Prize for Literature, Best Writing Award). He co-hosts the Aural Text show on 3RRR community radio and writes regularly for Crikey, The Drum Unleashed and elsewhere.

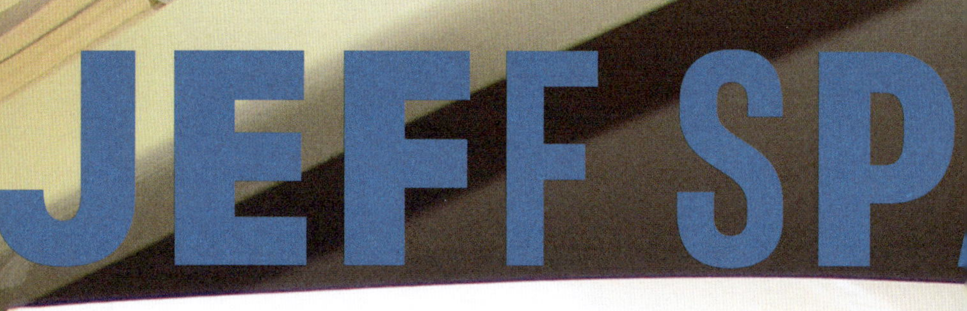
JEFF SP
72
overland
Registered for posting as a publication, Category B.
stories
features
poetry
$2

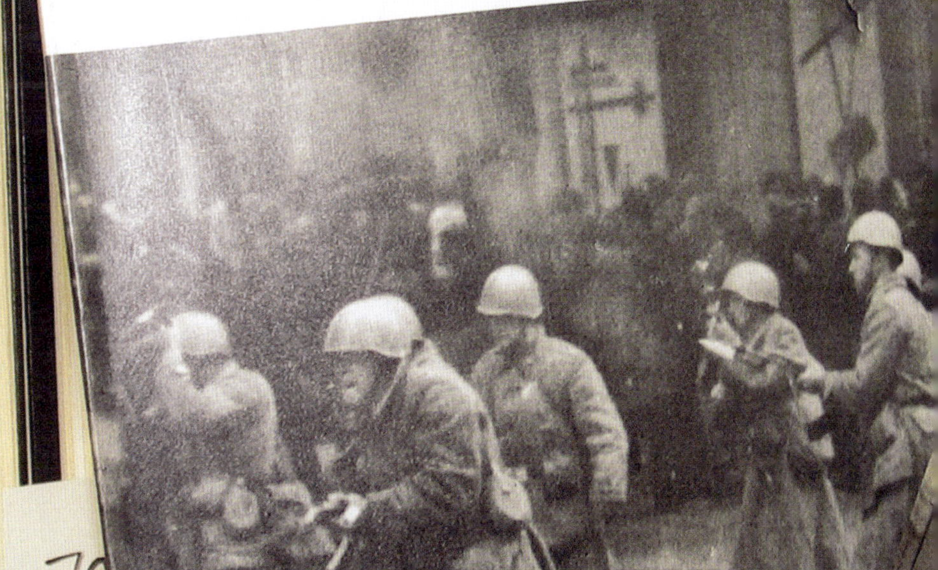

First published in 2010 by
The Council of Trustees of the
National Gallery of Victoria
180 St Kilda Road
Melbourne, Victoria 3004, Australia
www.ngv.vic.gov.au

Published for the exhibition
Harrell Fletcher: The Sound We Make Together (Melbourne)
The Ian Potter Centre:
NGV Australia at Federation Square,
11 September 2010 – 30 January 2011

National Library of Australia
Cataloguing-in-Publication entry:

Baker, Alex.
Harrell Fletcher : The Sound We Make Together (Melbourne) /Alex Baker.
1st ed.
9780724103324 (pbk.)
Fletcher, Harrell–Exhibitions.
Performance art–Exhibitions.
Other Authors/Contributors:
National Gallery of Victoria.
700.904

Editor: Dianne Waite
Designer: Dirk Hiscock
Photography: Selina Ou
Publications Coordinator Megan Patty
Publications Manager: Jasmin Chua
Pre-press: Justine Frost
CTP and printing: Adams Print
Cover stock: Enviro Board 335gsm
Text stock: Laser Offset 110gsm

The views expressed in this publication are those of the authors and do not necessarily reflect those of the NGV or the publisher.

10 9 8 7 6 5 4 3 2 1

ARROW